The Vegetarian Mother and Baby Book

Completely Revised and Updated

ROSE ELLIOT

Pantheon Books
New York

ROSE ELLIOT'S ASTROLOGICAL SERVICE

As well as being a cookbook writer, Rose Elliot is also a qualified astrologer and practices as a consultant, writes columns for magazines, and, together with her husband Robert, runs Rose Elliot Horoscopes. Rose says that the unique blend of qualities which make every baby special can be seen in the astrological birth chart. No one knows why this is so, but her clients have written many times to confirm that this is true and a horoscope really does reveal the character. The pattern the planets make at the time of birth shows the energies your child will use to develop his or her character. For instance, it shows the differences between the gentle, sensitive Piscean child and the robust, adventurous Aries; the deeply emotional Scorpio who keeps his feelings hidden and the open Sagittarian who can't keep anything secret; the talkative Gemini and the practical, down-to-earth Capricorn with much ambition and determination to succeed. It is fascinating and helpful to know in advance the way your child's character is likely to evolve. This is just what Rose Elliot's Children's Horoscopes will tell you. Rose has written them to help you understand your child's potential and the best ways you can help to draw it out. If you would like to order a horoscope, please write to:

Rose Elliot Horoscopes, PO Box 16, Eastleigh, Hampshire, SO50 5YP, United Kingdom, enclosing your child's name, date, time and place of birth, and the mailing address, and also either a check/postal order or MasterCard/Visa details including name and expiration date of card. The cost in 1996 for an Astrological Profile for children (or for adults) is £15 in the UK and £17 elsewhere.

CONTENTS

Author's Note

Like all writers of books about babies, I had to face the problem of what pronoun to use when referring to the baby. Determined not to be sexist, I started by calling the baby 'it'. But that didn't sound right, so in line with a number of recent babycare books – and since I myself have three daughters – I eventually settled on 'she'. To mothers of baby sons, I apologize if this seems inappropriate, and hope you'll mentally read 'he' instead.

Acknowledgments

I'd like to express my love and gratitude to my mother, Joan Hodgson, whose mothering was the pattern and model for my own; and to my husband and three daughters, without whom this book certainly wouldn't have been written. My grateful thanks, too, to all the people who have encouraged and helped me in writing this book: to the Vegetarian Society (UK) for getting me started, and to Fontana (and especially Helen Fraser) for publishing the original UK edition of *Rose Elliot's Vegetarian Mother and Baby Book*; also to Vivienne Schuster, my agent at that time; to Dr Alan Long for advice on nutrition; to Juliet Gellately for information on soy milk; and to Gill Thorn, my birth counselor when I had Claire, and dear friend ever since, for reading through both the original and the current manuscript and making many valuable suggestions. My special thanks, too, to Wendy Wolf and Juliet Annan of Pantheon for making the first US edition possible, and particularly for all their ideas and suggestions, many of which appear in this new US edition. I would also like to extend my very grateful thanks to all those involved with this present edition: to Polly Powell and Barbara Dixon of HarperCollins and my agent Barbara Levy for their enthusiasm and support; to Kelly Davis for her inspired editing.

PART I

NUTRITION AND BABYCARE

Introduction

The question of diet is an especially important one for vegetarian or vegan parents and parents-to-be. If you are vegetarian or vegan and pregnant, or planning to start a family in the near future, you may be wondering whether such a diet can supply all the nutrients necessary for producing a healthy baby. Indeed, you - or if not you, probably your mother or mother-in-law - may also wonder whether such a diet is actually nutritious enough to sustain you and your partner over a long period of time.

To set your mind at rest right away, the answer to all these questions is yes, and it may encourage you to know that vigorous, lively fifth-generation vegetarian and vegan babies are now being born. It is, however, helpful to have access to a few crucial facts about nutrition, and particularly important for a pregnant or about-to-be pregnant vegetarian or vegan, or one who is caring for a baby or toddler.

I wrote the first edition of this book – *Rose Elliot's Vegetarian Baby Book* – for the Vegetarian Society in the UK, in response to many requests for such information following the birth of my third daughter, Claire. This simple volume was then expanded to become *The Vegetarian Mother and Baby Book* and was published by Pantheon.

An American edition followed, with many new features, such as sample vegan and vegetarian menus, quick and easy meal plans for after the birth, lunches which a baby and parent can share, and menus for toddlers' lunches and dinners. The 'baby book', as I refer to it, became one of my most popular books and the one which provokes far and away the largest number of letters from readers, sometimes accompanied by delightful photographs of smiling, healthy babies.

Now the time has come for a new edition, and the book has been transformed yet again. In this hardback edition, I decided to blend together the best of both the original UK edition and the later US edition, with much new information and fresh ideas and recipes to bring it right up to date. It has also been given another new name to reflect more completely its content: *The Vegetarian Mother and Baby Book, Completely Revised and Updated*. I hope that it will prove to be as useful and well-loved as its predecessors. It comes with my love and best wishes to vegetarian and vegan mothers (and fathers) who read it, and their babies and toddlers.

How a Vegetarian Diet Can Supply All the Nutrients Needed for Health

First, perhaps it would be helpful to define what is usually meant by the words 'vegetarian' and 'vegan'. A vegetarian diet generally means one that excludes meat, fish, and poultry, and products derived from these, such as meat stock and fats (for example, lard, drippings, suet) and gelatin, but includes eggs, milk and dairy products. A vegan diet is stricter and excludes all animal products (including honey).

As I have already said, both these diets can supply all the nutrients necessary for health. Indeed, there are many people who would go further and say that not only can they do this, but they are also healthier than a traditional meat diet because they bypass the saturated fat and unwanted hormones, antibiotics, and other undesirable additives commonly found in meat. Nevertheless, whatever we vegetarians think about eating animals, if we're fair-minded, we have to admit that meat and fish are concentrated sources of some essential nutrients. Although adequate amounts of these can be found in most vegetarian foods, on the whole we do not have such concentrated sources. So, while a meat eater can be adequately nourished without knowing much about nutrition, if you're a vegetarian or vegan, it's helpful to know a few simple facts so that you can be sure to base your diet on the most nutritious foods. If you do this, the chances are you'll end up far healthier and more full of energy than any meat eater!

The Essential Nutrients:
What They Are and Where to Find Them

This section gives a brief summary of the essential nutrients and their main sources. The recommended daily dietary allowance (RDA) for each nutrient is given on p. 83 and you can find out the precise quantities obtained from different foods by consulting the nutrient charts on pp. 84-5. Finally, the chart on p. 86 shows how the various nutrients add up over a typical day's eating.

Protein

This is the first thing most people worry about when they start thinking about vegetarian nutrition, which is understandable, since a vegetarian diet excludes two major sources of protein, meat and fish. However, getting sufficient protein is not such a problem as people imagine. In fact if a vegetarian diet contains sufficient B vitamins and calcium, it will almost certainly contain adequate amounts of protein as well, because the foods that contain these nutrients are also good (if in some instances unconventional) sources of protein. It's rather a case of "If you look after the calcium and B vitamins, the protein will look after itself"! Cereals, for instance, which are vital sources of the B vitamins thiamin, riboflavin, and niacin, also contain a significant amount of protein, which adds up over the course of the day. The same applies to legumes. Milk, yogurt, and cheese, which are rich in both calcium and B vitamins, are, as we all know, high in protein. Vegans, of course, do not eat dairy products, but, again, if they take in adequate amounts of B vitamins and calcium (as explained on pp. 8-10 and 13), their diet, too, will contain sufficient protein.

It is sometimes stated that, in order to get sufficient protein, vegetarians need to mix proteins of different types or 'complementary proteins' – for example, grains and legumes – at the same meal. This is not so, as the following 1993 statement from the American Dietetic Association explains:

Plant sources of protein alone can provide adequate amounts of the essential and non-essential amino acids, assuming that dietary protein sources from plants are reasonably varied and that caloric intake is sufficient to meet energy needs. Whole grains, legumes, vegetables, seeds, and nuts all contain essential and non-essential amino acids. Conscious combining of these foods within a given meal, as the complementary protein dictum suggests, is unnecessary. Additionally, soy protein has been shown to be nutritionally equivalent in protein value to proteins of animal origin and thus can serve as the sole source of protein intake if desired.

Fiber

Fiber is not a nutrient, but it is vital to health. It is the structural part of fruits, vegetables, and cereals: the cellulose, woods and gums that hold them together. Fiber serves as a kind of rationing device, beginning in the mouth, because it has to be chewed, and there's a limit to the amount of chewing anyone can do. So you might say fiber is nature's way of preventing us from becoming fat, and certainly people on 'primitive' diets containing a high amount of fiber are naturally slim. But the role of fiber doesn't end there. Just as we had to bite our way through the fiber to eat the food, so our digestive juices have to work their way through the fiber in order to extract all the goodness mixed up with it. Therefore, our bodies are able to cope with the nutrients gradually, as they're drawn out. The whole process is methodical and systematic. Then, as the fiber travels along the digestive tract, it absorbs liquid and becomes bulky, like a sponge. Thus the muscles of the intestine can get a good grip and move its contents along smoothly, quickly, and efficiently.

Lack of fiber

If the fiber is taken out of foods, these natural safeguards are lost. Sugar is perhaps the ultimate example of this. In its natural state sugar is found in fruits and vegetables and in particular in sugar cane and sugar beet, a tough root. If it wasn't for modern refining methods, it would be impossible to eat more than a sprinkling of sugar even if you chewed all day long. As it is, it's easy to eat a bar of chocolate or several cookies and hardly notice it.

So, instead of the digestive system having to work its way slowly through the fiber to ease the goodness out, with refined foods this natural regulator has been eliminated, and the nutrients get into the bloodstream quickly, in a flood. The body has to take emergency action, releasing a great deal of insulin to digest the sugar. While this may be all right occasionally, there is growing evidence to suggest that repeatedly straining the body in this way can upset the delicate mechanism that controls the flow of insulin, resulting in diabetes.

Finally, of course, lack of fiber means that when the food passes through the digestive tract, there is nothing to hold the water and provide the spongelike action. Without the softening, water-holding properties of fiber, waste matter is dry and hard and more difficult to move along the intestine. It tends to break up and get stuck in pockets along the way. This is one of the chief causes of diverticular disease, from which one in three people over the age of 60 suffer in affluent countries. Hard, dry waste matter also takes longer to pass through the bowel, which can lead to constipation. Some experts think that when the passage of fecal matter through the bowel is slow, toxins may be reabsorbed by the body and that this may be linked with the increase of cancer of the bowel in industrialized countries.

Increasing fiber intake

Foods high in fiber are legumes (including baked beans); all fruits and vegetables, but in particular carrots, apples, dried figs, and dried apricots, because of the capacity of the fiber in these to reabsorb water; nuts and seeds; and whole grains, such as whole wheat, brown rice, and millet. These are the foods that normally feature prominently in a vegetarian/vegan diet, which is usually more than adequate from the point of view of fiber. The only time when a vegetarian or vegan diet may be low in fiber is if it is based on processed convenience foods; white flour, pasta, and rice; and dairy products. A diet like this could also be lacking important vitamins, but can easily be improved by swapping white bread, rice and pasta for their whole wheat equivalents; by having whole wheat cereal or fruit, yogurt and wheat germ for breakfast; by including more fresh fruits and vegetables, starting with, perhaps, salad sandwiches or a large salad for lunch and a good serving of green vegetables (cooked or as a salad) as part of the evening meal.

The US Department of Agriculture recommends that adult diets contain an average of 25 g fiber per day (individual needs vary between 20 and 30 g per day). A vegetarian or vegan diet planned along the lines suggested in this book is unlikely to be deficient in fiber. For instance two slices of whole wheat bread supply 5 g of fiber; a medium-sized (5-ounce) baked potato supplies 3 g; 8 ounces of baked beans provide 16.5 g of fiber; and five figs yield 18.4 g.

Fat

The question of fat is tied up with that of fiber, because if you think of fat in its most natural form it is contained within the kernels of grains, nuts, and seeds, or bound up with fiber in vegetables and fruits, such as the avocado. These polyunsaturated fats are essential to health; they are necessary for the absorption of the fat-soluble vitamins – A, D, E, and K. Of course we also add fat to our food in the form of milk, butter, egg yolk, margarine, and vegetable oils, and most people in developed countries eat far more fat than necessary. Calories from fat often make up about 40 percent of total calorie intake, whereas some experts believe the ideal would be nearer 10 percent. This is a very difficult level to reach and would mean rather sparse meals of a kind most people probably don't want to eat. Nonetheless, most of us can cut our fat intake a little, with beneficial results, by using a skim, lowfat, or soy milk in place of ordinary milk, using nonfat or soy yogurt and lowfat cheeses, and cutting down on the amount of fat we put on bread.

Some vegetarian sources of protein, such as cheese, nuts, and seeds, are quite high in fat but they are also concentrated sources of important nutrients and are used in small quantities: 1 to 2 ounces of nuts is an average serving, and is usually eaten along with fruit, legumes or vegetables, which contain no fat. However, vegetarians do need to be careful not to take in too much fat through the over-generous use of dairy products. Cheddar-type cheeses, for instance, are high in fat (the reduced-fat ones are recommended), but they are also concentrated, so 1^1/2 to 2 ounces makes a generous serving. Compare this with the amount of meat that would make a satisfactory portion. Because of this, and the other valuable nutrients contained in cheese, it is an important food for lacto-vegetarians.

Using fat wisely

Regarding the best type of fat to use, and whether butter is preferable to margarine, I believe that the most important thing is to cut one's consumption of all fats, whether they are added to foods or eaten 'hidden' in cakes and pastries. I use (relatively) cheap blended olive oil for all sautéing and the cold-pressed corn, safflower or soybean oil is also good on salads because of its high vitamin E content (see p. 11). However, for deep frying it is necessary to use a peanut or soybean oil that is not cold-pressed (though ideally deep frying should be kept to a minimum). At the table, I use a good-quality non-hydrogenated pure vegetable margarine (from the health food store) or butter.

The reason for my choice of fats is that when vegetable oils are heated, as happens during the refining process and in the making of margarine, the chemical structure of the molecules is altered, and the valuable fatty acids, which the body needs, are altered and become trans fatty acids, which are harmful to health. There appears to be a link between high intake of trans fatty acids and some cancers, just as there appears to be a link between high intake of saturated fat and heart disease. Forewarned is forearmed. Fats such as butter, olive oil, peanut oil, and soybean oil, on the other hand, are chemically more stable when heated, so I prefer to use them for cooking.

However, I must stress again that the most important point is to reduce your overall fat intake. This does not mean giving up delicious things like French fries, avocados, or strawberries and cream; it just means balancing them with plenty of cereals, legumes, vegetables, and fresh fruits. That way you can have your fat and still stay slim and healthy.

Vitamins

Vitamins are substances that are essential for good health; a deficiency in any of them can result in a number of minor ailments and impaired health and growth, especially in children. The vitamins fall into two groups, those that are soluble in fat and can be stored in the body and those that are soluble in water.

Water-Soluble Vitamins

The water-soluble vitamins are the B vitamins and vitamin C. Because they dissolve in water, they have to be taken daily and can easily be lost or destroyed through contact with air, sunlight, heat, and water.

B Vitamins

There are 13 B vitamins, and they are grouped together because they are interdependent. They tend to occur in the same foods and, with the exception of B12, you shouldn't take a supplement of an individual B vitamin, except under medical supervision, as this can upset the delicate balance. Getting adequate quantities of most of the B vitamins presents no problems to either vegetarians or vegans, although vegans do need to keep an eye on their riboflavin (vitamin B2) which vegetarians can get from dairy produce.

Vitamin B1 (Thiamin)

Thiamin is needed by the body for the release of energy from starch and sugar. A deficiency of this vitamin causes poor appetite and general lack of well-being. The best sources of thiamin are brewers' yeast, yeast extract, wheat germ, fortified breakfast cereals, and Brazil nuts and peanuts (both raw and roasted, although raw ones contain more thiamin). Oats, millet, whole wheat bread, legumes and peas are also good sources, and green vegetables, dried fruits, and (for lactovegetarians)

milk, yogurt, and cheese supply useful amounts. A vegetarian or vegan diet planned along the lines suggested in this book will contain more than enough thiamin to meet daily requirements.

Vitamin B2 (Riboflavin)

Like thiamin, riboflavin is needed for the release of energy from food, as well as for the absorption of iron. It is necessary for the proper functioning of the brain and resistance to infection. A lack of riboflavin can cause poor appetite and sores at the corners of the mouth and nose. Best sources are brewers' yeast, yeast extract, wheat germ, milk and milk products. Millet, whole wheat pasta and fortified breakfast cereals (a 1-ounce serving provides a quarter of the recommended daily allowance), eggs, leafy green vegetables and mushrooms also contain reasonable amounts. Other vegetables, whole wheat bread and oats, and fresh and dried fruits all contribute to the day's total. Most people get a high percentage of their riboflavin from milk and milk products; vegans, and vegetarians who only eat small quantities of dairy products, need to take care to choose foods which provide this vitamin.

Vitamin B3
(Niacin/Nicotinic Acid)

Niacin has a function similar to that of riboflavin, and a deficiency can cause similar symptoms, including mouth ulcers. It is found in brewers' yeast and yeast extract; wheat germ; whole wheat bread; whole grains, especially millet and whole wheat pasta; legumes; cheese; avocados; dried apricots, dates, and figs; vegetables, especially mushrooms, dark green leafy vegetables, and asparagus; and almonds and walnuts. Peanuts are one of the richest sources of all. Although wholegrain cereals are a good source of niacin, it is not certain how much of this is available to the body, because it is in bound form. In one survey of vegan mothers, levels of niacin were found to be well above average, probably because of the prominence of legumes and yeast extracts in their diet.

Pantothenic Acid

This vitamin is very widely distributed and is found in all foods except fats, sugar, and spirits. It is needed for the release of energy and for the proper functioning of the adrenal glands. If you are getting enough of the other B vitamins, you will be getting enough pantothenic acid as well.

Vitamin B6 (Pyridoxine)

This vitamin is needed for the metabolism of protein and for the formation of blood. Lack of vitamin B6 can cause irritability, depression, sore mouth, and skin and scalp irritation, and may contribute to heart disease and diabetes. Best sources are brewers' yeast, yeast extract and wheat germ; whole wheat bread, whole grains and fortified breakfast cereals; legumes and sprouted legumes; nuts, especially Brazil nuts and walnuts; dark green leafy vegetables; corn; cabbage; avocado; and dried and fresh fruits, especially bananas and pineapple. Vitamin B6 is also in eggs, milk, and milk products. A diet along the lines described on pages 17-19 will meet the requirements for this vitamin. When vegetables are boiled, vitamin B6 leaches out into the cooking water, but the loss of this nutrient can be avoided by using just enough water to be absorbed during the cooking, or by straining off and re-using the cooking water, or by using other methods of cooking, such as stir frying or steaming, or by serving fruits and vegetables raw.

Folic Acid (Folate)

Folic acid is used by the body, along with vitamin B12, for cell division, and a deficiency may cause a form of anemia. All foods except fats, sugar, and spirits contain some folic acid, but for vegetarians the richest sources are brewers' yeast, yeast extract, and wheat germ. Whole wheat bread and whole grains are also valuable sources, as are most vegetables (especially dark green leafy ones, asparagus, and sprouted legumes) and fruits (especially oranges and bananas). Nuts (especially walnuts and almonds) and pumpkin seeds are also good sources. For lactovegetarians, cheese, milk, and eggs also contribute. Folic acid is sensitive to heat and light, and 50 to 90 percent of the folic acid in vegetables can be destroyed by cooking, so serve plenty of salads; stir fry or cook vegetables carefully for as short a time as possible in the smallest quantity of water, and save the water for use in soups and sauces.

It is particularly important to boost your intake of folic acid both before and during pregnancy and while breastfeeding. (For more on this, see p. 39.)

Vitamin B12

Vitamin B12 functions similarly to vitamins B1, B2, and B3, but in addition it is needed for the production of bone marrow. A deficiency can cause pernicious anemia. The major sources of B12 are meat and dairy products, although it can also be manufactured by yeast-like microorganisms, algae, bacteria and molds. Vegetarians can get some B12 from eggs and dairy products, and both vegetarians and vegans from B12-fortified foods such as most yeast extracts, some breakfast cereals, and some soy milks (read the labels). Vegetarians and vegans who are not getting much from these sources might be well advised to take a supplement.

Vitamin C

Vitamin C is important for resistance to infection and is needed for the absorption of iron, tissue repair, and normal growth. Vitamin C is present in many fresh fruits and vegetables, but it is easily lost through exposure to air, heat, and water. However, a normal vegetarian or vegan diet, with its abundance of fruits and vegetables, is unlikely to be lacking in vitamin C. One half-cup serving of orange juice supplies daily needs, and raw cabbage, cauliflower, watercress, and tomatoes are other good sources. Cooked cabbage and potatoes also contain useful amounts.

Fat-Soluble Vitamins

Vitamins A, D, E, and K dissolve in fat. They can therefore be stored in the body. Vitamins A and D can be toxic in high doses, so supplements should only be taken at the recommended levels.

Vitamin A

There are two forms of this vitamin, one that is found in dairy products and fortified margarine and another, called beta-carotene, that is found in many dark green, orange, and yellow fruits and vegetables. Beta-carotene is converted into vitamin A by the body. Vitamin A is essential for the proper functioning of the eyes and the mucous membranes throughout the body, as well as for proper growth and resistance to infection. A deficiency increases the risk of infections in the throat, eyes, and skin, also bronchitis. Vitamin A is found in spinach and other dark green leafy vegetables and in orange fruits and vegetables, especially carrots (3 ounces of carrots more than supply the day's requirements). Other good sources are butter, eggs, cheese, and fortified margarines. A normal vegetarian or vegan diet is not likely to be short of this vitamin.

Vitamin D

The body needs vitamin D in order to use calcium efficiently. This vitamin is obtained both from foods and by the action of sunlight on the skin. It is present in few foods and, with the exception of margarine and some breakfast cereals (which are fortified with vitamin D), they are all animal products. The richest source is cod liver oil, which is obviously unsuitable for both vegetarians and vegans, also eggs, butter, milk (including evaporated and fortified skim milk – check the label), cheese, yogurt, and cottage cheese.

Some experts believe that you can get all the vitamins you need by the action of sunlight on the skin but, unless you live in a very sunny part of the world, it's best not to rely on this source. People with dark skins cannot absorb vitamin D from sunshine, so they can become deficient in vitamin D. Many experts recommend a daily vitamin D supplement for everyone, whether vegetarian or not, and I think this is sensible advice, especially for young children and old people.

But if you are taking any general vitamin tablets, check whether these contain vitamin D before adding any extra to your diet; and if you're taking a vitamin D supplement, be careful to measure the dose precisely, because excessive vitamin D is toxic.

Vitamin E

Vitamin E improves general vitality and is important for the functioning of the heart. It may help to avoid atherosclerosis (hardening of the arteries) and high blood pressure. It is also said to increase fertility, help prevent varicose veins, and improve the body's ability to heal itself. The best sources of vitamin E are wheat germ; cold-pressed vegetable oils, especially corn, safflower, and wheat germ oil; almonds; peanuts; and Brazil nuts. Eggs, butter, cheese, whole wheat flour and bread, oats, rice, and millet are also quite good sources, as are apples, bananas, cantaloupes, oranges, and grapefruit. A vegetarian diet, with its regular use of whole grains, nuts, and seeds, is unlikely to be short of this vitamin.

Vitamin K

Necessary for blood clotting and to prevent excess loss of blood after injury, vitamin K can be manufactured by the intestinal bacteria, except when the process is inhibited as a result of taking antibiotics. (Eating active yogurt afterwards will help restore the intestinal bacteria so that they can do their job.) Vitamin K is found in leafy green vegetables, tomatoes, soybean oil, egg yolks, and seaweed. A daily serving of leafy green vegetables will make sure that you have an adequate amount of this vitamin.

Minerals

There are 15 minerals that are essential for the health of the body, and five more that are thought to be necessary. The most important are iron, calcium, magnesium, phosphorus, potassium, and sodium.

Iron

Iron is needed for the formation of blood and for carrying oxygen in the blood; lack of iron can cause anemia. Iron deficiency in women is one of the most common problems in the American diet but scientific studies have shown that vegetarians and vegans are no more likely to suffer from this than meat eaters. In a vegetarian diet, iron is obtained from legumes (soybeans and lentils are excellent sources); soy flour and whole grain cereals, especially whole wheat bread and millet (which contains the most iron of the grains); nuts and seeds; dark green vegetables; and dried fruits (apricots and prunes are particularly good sources). Brewers' yeast, molasses, and wheat germ are concentrated sources of iron, and egg yolk is a useful source, too, for vegetarians who eat eggs and dairy products. A vegetarian or vegan diet planned along the lines suggested on pp. 17-19 will meet the recommended iron levels.

Not all the iron in food can be used by the body, since other components in the diet prevent it from being absorbed, and the RDA is set high to allow for this. Many iron-rich foods, such as nuts, wheat, peas, and beans, also contain a substance called phytic acid, which combines with iron and prevents full absorption. This effect is lessened when iron-rich foods are eaten along with a source of vitamin C, such as orange juice. So choose bread that has risen in preference to soda breads, since well-risen whole wheat bread contains less phytic acid, and that is further broken down in the baking process. In addition, the processes of soaking, sprouting, and cooking legumes help to break down phytic acid, as does soaking oats overnight for breakfast muesli. It is helpful to know that blanched almonds and skinned peanuts contain less phytic acid than those with the skins on. And since it's the bran in whole wheat flour that contains most of the phytic acid, it's best not to add extra bran to your meals, except under medical supervision. In any case this is usually unnecessary under normal conditions because a vegetarian diet is naturally high in fiber.

Fortunately, research has shown that after a time the body adapts to a vegetarian diet, so that phytic acid is digested lower down in the intestine, after minerals such as iron and zinc have been absorbed. Apparently this adaptation is accomplished quickly, and if you are already eating some high-fiber foods, such as whole wheat bread, your body is probably already making the change.

If you're worried about your iron level, choose an iron-rich grain such as millet or whole wheat pasta in preference to rice; almonds, preferably blanched; and pumpkin seeds. Concentrate on legumes that are highest in iron – lentils and soybeans – either cooked or sprouted. Have nibbles of dried fruit, add a little soy flour to your cooking where possible, and sprinkle nutritional yeast flakes over your food. You can also boost your iron level by taking some blackstrap molasses daily, straight from the spoon if you like the flavor, dissolved in milk, mixed with a little honey; or in compotes, cookies, and bread (see recipes on pp. 137, 138 and 147). You can also drink prune juice, which is much more palatable than it sounds (especially with a shot of soda water), or use it to moisten your breakfast cereal (it's good with muesli). See p. 12 for more iron-boosting ideas.

Calcium

Calcium is needed for the health of bones, skin, and teeth, and for the functioning of the heart. It is also involved in blood-clotting. The richest sources of calcium are milk, cheese, and yogurt, and it's not difficult for lactovegetarians to obtain enough from these sources. Even a vegetarian eating a diet that is fairly low in dairy products, with just, say, $1\,^1/2$ cups of milk or yogurt during the day, can easily reach the RDA by including, for instance, 6 ounces of cooked broccoli and a few dried figs, which are good sources. Vegans would be well advised to use a calcium-enriched soy milk for drinking and making yogurt and to include a calcium-rich green leafy vegetable and some figs in their daily diet if possible. These foods, together with the grains, whole wheat bread, nuts, fruits, legumes, and vegetables that make up the day's meals, should ensure that your needs are met. The evidence is that, although vegans consume less calcium in their food, their bodies use it and store it more efficiently than those of meat eaters.

Phosphorus

Phosphorus is needed, together with calcium, for the formation and health of teeth and bones. It is present in many foods: milk, eggs, cereals, nuts, fruits, and vegetables, and there is no problem for either vegans or vegetarians in getting enough of this mineral.

Magnesium

Magnesium is needed for healthy bones and teeth and also for the process of drawing energy from carbohydrate foods. The best sources of magnesium for vegetarians and vegans are almonds, Brazil nuts, wheat germ, and peanuts; soy flour and soybeans, millet, and oats. There is also some in dried and fresh fruit and in leafy green vegetables, and some in whole wheat bread, which, in a balanced diet, all adds up over the course of the day to more than the recommended daily level. However, this is another mineral that is affected by the presence of phytic acid, as explained on p. 12. Because it is water-soluble, magnesium may be lost if you throw away the cooking water from boiled vegetables, although it is not damaged by heat, so fried, broiled, and baked vegetables retain their full amount. A normal vegetarian or vegan diet provides plentiful supplies of this mineral.

Potassium and Sodium

Potassium and sodium together control the fluid balance throughout the organs and tissues of the body. The ratio of potassium to sodium is higher in the muscles, organs and soft tissues of the body, whereas sodium predominates in the blood plasma and interstitial fluids. The better each of these minerals predominates in its own area, the better our health is likely to be.

Both sodium and potassium occur naturally in foods, but we also add sodium to our diet in the form of salt. For this reason, and because the foods rich in potassium are fresh raw fruit and vegetables, which do not figure prominently in many people's diet, most people have too much sodium and too little potassium. This means that gradually the proper sodium-potassium balance in their body breaks down, and all the vital organs, especially the liver and heart, can eventually suffer. Too little potassium can also contribute to tiredness, because potassium helps in the process of carrying oxygen to the cells.

A vegetarian diet is usually high in potassium because of the fresh fruit and vegetables it normally contains. There is also potassium in wheat germ, legumes, and whole grains, so there is no problem in obtaining enough of this mineral. You can further improve your diet by being sparing in your use of salt to season foods and by avoiding salty manufactured foods, especially potato chips and similar snacks.

Trace Elements

Trace elements are substances known to be present in the body and to be used in conjunction with other minerals and vitamins. Research into their subtle interaction with other substances and their function and importance is continuing, but deficiencies have been noted in a variety of physical and mental disorders.

Zinc

Zinc is vitally important in the formation of DNA and RNA (the hereditary materials of all organisms). A deficiency of zinc often manifests itself as white flecks on the fingernails and skin problems, such as eczema and acne. Make a point of including in your diet foods that are rich in this mineral. The best sources of zinc for vegetarians are wheat germ, whole wheat bread and other grains, and nuts and seeds, especially pumpkin seeds. Legumes, either cooked or sprouted; green leafy vegetables, especially spinach; corn, peas, mushrooms, fresh asparagus, mango, and nutritional yeast flakes are also good sources. Cheese, milk, and yogurt can supply useful amounts for lactovegetarians. Although intake of this trace element needs watching, studies show that vegetarians and vegans consume as much if not more zinc than meat eaters. Phytic acid (see p. 12) was once thought to interfere with the body's ability to absorb zinc, but recent research shows that this only happens in the presence of large quantities of calcium.

Manganese

Another vitally important trace element, manganese is abundant in nuts, peas, beans, and whole grains but the phytic acid that is also present in these foods interferes with its absorption to some degree, although how much is not yet known. The best sources are whole wheat bread, wheat germ, almonds, Brazil nuts, cashews, peanuts, and walnuts. Dried figs, dates, peaches, and apricots are also good sources, and brewers' yeast supplies some. Potatoes, bananas, and fresh fruit and vegetables also contribute. A vegetarian or vegan diet planned along the lines suggested will not be deficient in this mineral.

Iodine

Iodine is necessary for the proper functioning of the thyroid gland. The main sources are seafoods (including seaweeds and thus vegetarian jelling agents, such as agar and gelose), and iodized table salt. Milk is also a surprisingly rich source in the US because of the iodine in cattle feed and other substances used in milk production. Getting sufficient quantities of this trace element is unlikely to be a problem for either vegans or vegetarians.

Selenium

The importance of this trace element was discovered in 1973. It works with vitamin E to protect the body from the harmful effects of oxidation by free radicals and helps synthesize antibodies. Best vegetarian sources are Brazil nuts, molasses, wheat germ, sunflower seeds, whole wheat bread, and dairy produce.

Vegetarians and vegans do not have a problem with selenium because of lack of animal produce; if there is a problem it is geographical. This is because the selenium content of foods depends on the amount of selenium in the soil in which they are grown. Some areas of the world are deficient in selenium. These include north, central and eastern Canada and extreme south-eastern areas of the US, as well as China, Finland, and New Zealand. A selenium supplement is recommended for people living in these areas.

Clearly, getting enough of the vital nutrients isn't a problem. Although people tend to worry about what may be lacking in a vegetarian or vegan diet, research is increasingly showing that this is the healthiest way of living, so let's stop worrying about deficiencies and look at the many advantages. For instance, vegetarians are five times less likely to be admitted to hospital than meat eaters and a vegetarian diet can significantly reduce the incidence of heart disease, cancer, hypertension, diabetes, and many other illnesses. In the next section we will see how it all works out in terms of meals.

Creating a Balanced Diet

If you've read this far and you're feeling quite confused by all the dietary requirements and their various possible sources, I don't blame you! It does seem complicated. But once you start thinking in terms of a day's meals, it gets easier. Dr Michael Klaper, a leading vegan doctor, has devised a daily guide which shows what to eat each day in order to get all the nutrients you need. This plan is actually vegan; for a vegetarian version, include a few dairy products instead of some of the legumes, grains or nuts.

Here's how you could use the daily nutrients guide (overleaf) to create a day's meal plan (include 1¹/₂ cups of milk or calcium-enriched soy milk, used throughout the day in drinks, on cereals, and so on):

Breakfast
Crunchy Muesli (made from rolled oats, wheat germ, chopped figs or dates, slivered almonds and pumpkin seeds);
whole wheat toast
or 1 ounce enriched whole wheat breakfast cereal

Lunch
Salad sandwiches, including 3-4 slices whole wheat bread and Hummus (p. 91), cheese or peanut butter
Orange

DAILY NUTRIENTS GUIDE			
FOOD GROUP	WHAT IT PROVIDES	SOME EXAMPLES	HOW OFTEN TO EAT
whole grains and potatoes	energy, protein, oils, vitamins and fiber	brown rice, corn, millet, barley, bulgur, buckwheat, oats, muesli, bread, pasta, and flour	2-4 servings daily
legumes	protein and oils	green peas, lentils, chick peas, kidney beans, baked beans, soy products (incl. soy milk, tofu, tempeh, and TVP)	1-2 servings daily
green and yellow vegetables	vitamins, minerals and protein	broccoli, Brussels sprouts, spinach, cabbage, carrots, sweet potatoes, squashes, and parsnips	1-3 servings daily
nuts and seeds	energy, protein, oils, calcium, trace elements	almonds, pumpkin seeds, walnuts, peanuts, sesame seeds, nut butters, tahini, and sunflower seeds	1-3 servings daily
fruit	energy, vitamins and minerals	all kinds	3-6 pieces daily
vitamin and mineral foods	trace elements and vitamin B12	(a) sea vegetables (b) B12-fortified foods (e.g. soy milk, TVP, breakfast cereals, soy 'meat' products)	1 serving of (a) and (b) 3 times per week

Note: The servings of nuts and seeds are 1 ounce and of sea vegetables just a sprinkling; all the others are about 4 ounces.

Dinner
Mediterranean Butter Bean Casserole
(p. 110) with brown rice or crusty whole
wheat bread and green salad or cooked
Brussels sprouts
Fresh fruit or Baked Apple with Raisins
(p. 145)

Snacks
Whole wheat toast with honey, yeast
extract, or peanut butter
Fresh fruit
Carrot or celery sticks or raw
cauliflower florets
Nuts and raisins

To see how the day's meal plan described above adds up to meet daily nutritional requirements, see the chart on p. 86.

Breakfast Ideas

- Fresh fruit compote, with a scattering of nuts; whole wheat toast
- Dried and Fresh Fruit Compote or Molasses Compote (p. 147) with yogurt or soy yogurt; whole wheat toast
- Fresh fruit; yogurt or soy yogurt; whole wheat toast
- Oatmeal; fruit juice; whole wheat toast
- Crunchy Muesli (p. 17); fruit juice; whole wheat toast

- Scrambled eggs or Scrambled Tofu (p. 125) on toast
- Tofu Potato Cakes (p. 125) or fried smoked tofu with fried tomatoes and mushrooms

Five-Star Foods

As you may have noticed, many of the foods I've mentioned appear over and over again as good sources of nutrients. So enriching your diet can be simple if you concentrate on these – what I call 'five-star foods'. They are:

- Fresh fruit and vegetable juices
- Whole grains, including brown rice, whole wheat bread, and wheat germ
- Nuts and seeds, especially sesame (and tahini), sunflower and pumpkin seeds, pistachios and almonds
- Yeast extract and nutritional yeast flakes
- Blackstrap molasses
- Legumes and products made from them, including soy milk, tofu and hummus
- Dried fruits, including apricots, peaches, dates, figs, prunes, and raisins

If you include these foods as often as you can, both in your meals and as extras and snacks to keep up your energy level, you will boost your nutrient intake and keep yourself and your growing baby in perfect health.

ONE WEEK'S VEGETARIAN/VEGAN MENUS
(Include 1-2 cups lowfat or fortified soy milk daily)
(Dishes marked * are suitable for freezing)

	LUNCH	DINNER
DAY 1	Focaccia with Avocado, Lettuce, and Tomato (p. 107) Fresh fruit or vegetable juice and/or fresh fruit	Bulgur with Broiled Vegetables (p. 112) Apricot Fool (p. 149) or fresh fruit
DAY 2	Leftover Bulgur with Broiled Vegetables (cold) with green salad or Country Salad (p. 96) Fresh juices and/or fruit	Microwave Risotto* (p. 113) and mixed salad with Vinaigrette (p. 88) Figs with Yogurt and Sesame Seeds (p. 148); or soy yogurt
DAY 3	Leftover Microwave Risotto (cold) with green salad; or Very Quick Lentil Soup* (p. 101) with Garlic Bread* (p. 108) Fresh juices and/or fruit	Pizza Giardinara* (p. 133) with mixed salad Fresh or Dried Fruit Compote (p. 147); or fresh fruit
DAY 4	Leftover Pizza Giardinara (hot or cold) and mixed Italian salad; or Hummus, Black Olive, and Cilantro Sandwiches (p. 107) Extra salad, fresh juices and/or fruit	Parsley and Onion Polenta* (p. 116) with tomato salad and oven-baked asparagus Strawberries
DAY 5	Tahini Dip (p. 90) with crudités Extra salad, fresh juices and/or fruit	Vegetable Stir-Fry with Tofu (p. 123) and brown rice Litchi and Kiwi Fruit Salad (p. 148) with slices of orange
DAY 6	Red Kidney Bean and Avocado Salad (p. 99) Extra salad, fresh juices and/or fruit	Onion and Olive Pie* (p. 130) with steamed green beans and mashed potatoes Blackberry Fool (p. 149) or fresh fruit
DAY 7	Leftover Onion and Olive Pie (hot or cold) and green salad Fresh juices and/or fruit	Fusilli with Zucchini, Parsley, and Lemon Sauce (p. 136) and mixed salad Sliced Peaches in Wine or Orange Juice (p. 149)

Diet for Pregnancy and Breastfeeding

A vegetarian or vegan diet, planned along the lines suggested here, will supply you with the basic nutrients you need for health and vitality. If you are improving your health in preparation for becoming pregnant in the future, it is strongly recommended that you change to a form of contraception other than the pill. The pill is known to affect the body's ability to metabolize vitamins B6, B2, B12, and folic acid, as well as zinc, copper, and iron.

Make sure your intake of vitamins B12 and D is adequate (see pp. 10 and 11) and that you are getting plenty of the other B vitamins, especially folic acid, as well as vitamin E and iron; eat the Five-Star Foods (p. 19) as often as possible – and relax and be happy!

During pregnancy, your daily nutrient requirements increase considerably: you need more iron for the growing baby and to enable your body to make more blood. Your need for folic acid is also increased, as it is for thiamin, niacin, and riboflavin, as well as vitamins A, C, and D. Your need for both protein and calcium also goes up. If your diet includes plenty of fresh fruit and vegetables, you will probably be getting more than enough of vitamins A and C, folic acid, and thiamin, although it would not hurt to boost your intake. Here are some easy ways to achieve this.

Protein

If you increase your intake of B vitamins, iron and calcium, as suggested below, you will automatically be getting more protein. Although dairy products and legumes (especially soy beans) are particularly good sources, even eating the odd extra slice of whole wheat bread adds protein to your diet.

Vitamins A and C

Eat plenty of fresh fruit and vegetables, especially the yellow and green ones, and red bell peppers and tomatoes. Try the Big C Fruit Salad (p. 148) for breakfast or at any time of day. One of the best ways to increase your intake of these vitamins is to make your own juice from fresh fruit and vegetables, preferably organically grown. A good juicer is not cheap but could be an excellent investment, because fresh fruit and vegetable juices are also a wonderful source of many other vitamins, minerals, and trace elements, including iron, calcium, zinc, and folic acid. Try apple, carrot, and celery juice as a basic, adding small quantities of parsley, spinach, cabbage, and raw beets if you wish.

Vitamin B1 (Thiamin)

Your need for thiamin is increased during pregnancy and you can get it from sunflower seeds, sesame seeds, pistachio nuts, Brazil nuts, whole grains, and yeast extract. Because it's so widespread, it's not difficult to get enough and a small (4-ounce) baked potato provides all the extra required in pregnancy.

Vitamin B2 (Riboflavin)

More riboflavin is needed during pregnancy and if you are a vegetarian and are taking extra milk, cheese, or yogurt for calcium, it will also supply more than enough extra riboflavin. A teaspoonful of yeast extract or 3 ounces of almonds is all a vegan needs to meet the extra demand. Other sources include nutritional yeast flakes, almonds, millet, wheat germ, barley, sesame and pumpkin seeds, hummus, dried fruit, molasses, soy beans, broccoli, spinach, greens, and mushrooms. Also, some breakfast cereals are fortified with it – a 1-ounce serving provides as much as a quarter of the suggested daily intake.

Niacin

Your niacin requirement is also increased during pregnancy, and peanuts, legumes, whole wheat bread, and fortified breakfast cereals are particularly good sources of this vitamin.

Folic Acid

Folic acid is essential for the baby's development, and supplements are recommended for all pregnant women during the first three months. It is important to boost your intake of this vitamin as much as you can both before and during your pregnancy and while breastfeeding. Many of the best natural sources of folic acid are vegan and some breakfast cereals are also fortified with it. Leafy green vegetables, particularly Brussels sprouts, broccoli, and spinach, and other vegetables, such as green beans, cauliflower, asparagus, and okra, are some of the best sources. It's always better if they are lightly cooked or served as salad or in whole wheat sandwiches. Fresh carrot and parsley juice is also a rich source of folic acid as well as of iron. Other sources are wheat germ, sunflower seeds, nuts, dates, beans (especially black-eyed peas), yeast extract, potatoes (especially baked and eaten with the skins), whole wheat bread, and fruit (particularly citrus fruits such as oranges and grapefruit).

Vitamin D

Normally the action of sunlight on the skin produces enough vitamin D. However, increased amounts are often recommended for pregnant women and breastfeeding mothers since it is needed for the utilization of calcium to form the baby's bones and for milk production. Take your doctor's advice, as too much vitamin D is toxic.

Calcium

Fresh vegetable juices are a useful source and broccoli, either raw or cooked, is very rich in it. Almonds and tofu prepared with calcium sulfate (check the label on the packet), and sesame seeds, tahini, and hummus made with tahini are other good sources of calci-

um, as well as milk, cheese, and yogurt. One sure way of getting enough is to take an extra $1^1/_2$ cups of milk or calcium-fortified soy milk or the equivalent in yogurt each day. The trace mineral boron helps your body to absorb calcium and plays an important role in avoiding osteoporosis. Make sure you have a good supply by eating plenty of fresh fruit and vegetables, particularly apples or apple juice.

Iron

The best sources of iron are dried fruits such as dried apricots and peaches, figs, dates, and prunes; nuts and seeds, particularly pistachio nuts, sunflower, pumpkin and sesame seeds, and blackstrap molasses. Lentils and other legumes, including tofu and soy milk, almonds, cashews, peanuts and peanut butter, hummus, cocoa, fortified breakfast cereals, red kidney beans, baked beans, oats, wheat, and wheat germ are also useful sources, as are dark green leafy vegetables and whole grains. Cook with these ingredients often.

To Avoid during Pregnancy

The US Food and Drug Administration advises that pregnant women avoid certain ripened soft cheeses such as Camembert, Brie, and blue-veined varieties which may contain high levels of listeria bacteria (Listeria monocytogenes). In very rare cases these bacteria can lead to an illness, listeriosis, which may result in miscarriage, stillbirth, or severe illness in the newborn baby.

Listeria bacteria have also been found in very small amounts in some prepared meals so, to be on the safe side, while you are pregnant, always reheat these thoroughly until they are piping hot. It's also best to make sure that any eggs you eat are well cooked, with the yolk and white solid, to avoid any risk of salmonella poisoning. Always wash vegetables and salads carefully to remove any soil and dirt which can carry toxoplasmosis infection; for the same reason, it is also best to make sure that any goat's milk you drink is pasteurized, sterilized or ultra-pasteurized.

Moderate alcohol consumption during pregnancy is not causing the concern it did a few years ago. However, alcohol does pass through the placenta and directly affects the baby, so the less you drink the better. Latest research suggests that there is no evidence of harm from drinking 2 units of alcohol a day and a maximum of 8 units a week.

Like alcohol, the stimulant caffeine, found in coffee, tea, cocoa, and cola-type drinks, also passes through the placenta to the baby. There have been concerns that it might lead to birth defects or miscarriages but studies have failed to give conclusive results.

Obviously, doctors advise against smoking, which is associated with low birth weight and crib death. It appears to have a worse effect later in pregnancy than in the first few weeks so it's never too late to cut down or give up.

While you are pregnant, any kind of medication must be considered very carefully and certainly only prescribed by a doctor who knows about your condition. This specifically includes aspirin, acetaminophen, and cold remedies which may contain them, and also vitamin supplements.

Although all sweeteners used in food and drink in the US are said to pose no risk to anyone, including pregnant women, I would also avoid them as they cross the placenta and are eliminated very slowly from fetal tissues.

Coping with Possible Problems in Pregnancy
Morning Sickness

When you first become pregnant, you may well feel slightly sick and not much like eating. During these early days you may find that there are only certain foods you want. Some people find milk, milky drinks, and yogurt helpful, while others turn to fresh fruits, salads, or whole wheat bread. Herb teas, especially peppermint, linden, and chamomile, can be useful.

For most people this stage only lasts for the first few weeks. If you do find you cannot eat normally, do not fear that your baby is being undernourished. Only if you are constantly sick and cannot keep anything down is it necessary to see your doctor, for in that case the baby could be at risk. Otherwise, just try to make sure that the foods you do eat are as whole and as natural as possible.

Once you know what is happening, you will probably find that you can control the nausea to some extent by having something to eat or drink as soon as you feel that strange, hungry, sick feeling. It is often helpful to avoid fatty foods and to eat little and often. Dry whole wheat toast or crackers might be helpful. You might also try eating a few dates or drinking a little apple or orange juice.

Food Cravings

The tendency to have odd cravings for foods in pregnancy is well known, and, within reason, these do not usually do any harm. If excessive, they may show a lack of some mineral, particularly iron (take medical advice), but minor food cravings are normal and, in my opinion, are to be indulged if possible, for they'll pass as the pregnancy progresses.

Heartburn

If you are suffering from heartburn (usually caused by the growing baby pressing against your stomach), it may help if you eat frequent small meals and cut out fatty foods as much as possible. Also eating concentrated starches (potatoes, bread, brown rice, and other grains) at the same time as you eat concentrated protein (cheese, eggs, dairy products) can help. Plan for a starch meal, which can include nuts, seeds, and all the fresh vegetables you want, plus the 'starchy' fruits (dates, dried fruit, bananas, and grapes); and a meal based on protein, nuts, and seeds, and all kinds of vegetables (except potatoes) and fruits (except the starchy ones just mentioned, though raisins are fine). Legumes are half-and-half protein-carbohydrate but they are best considered as starches in this context.

Constipation

A tendency towards constipation can be eased by increasing your intake of high-fiber foods: whole wheat bread, legumes (especially red kidney beans), nuts, fresh vegetables (including potatoes and beets), and fruit (especially raspberries). If you are also suffering from hemorrhoids, try to include buckwheat (see p. 112) in your diet as often as possible since this food contains rutin, a natural remedy for hemorrhoids and also for varicose veins.

Excessive Weight Gain

A close check will be kept on your weight during pregnancy. There is no reason why a vegetarian diet should be any more fattening than a conventional one, but pregnancy is a time when many women find they gain extra pounds very easily. If you find that your weight is increasing too rapidly, you would be wise to concentrate on the low-calorie high-protein foods, such as cottage and pot cheese, yogurt, tofu, legumes, wheat germ, and skim milk, with liberal amounts of fresh vegetables and fruit.

Many people are now questioning the wisdom of restricting weight gain too drastically during pregnancy. I rather go along with this view. Some reserves of fat (but not too many!) are helpful when it comes to the demands upon your body of breastfeeding; they can also help you weather the general stresses and strains of the early days with a young baby. And if you breastfeed for at least six months, you will almost certainly find that this extra weight just melts away even though you are, quite rightly, eating more than normal. But you do have to be patient while your food

stores, in the form of body fat, are gradually used up in the production of milk for your baby. Then, with any luck, you'll find you're back to normal; if not, then when breastfeeding is over is the time to adjust your diet a bit, as described above, in order to help you lose those last few pounds.

With all these "dos" and "don'ts", and the tests which are now commonplace, it's easy to forget that pregnancy is a perfectly normal, natural, healthy state. You can lose confidence in the ability of the human body to function normally without intervention and to produce healthy, beautiful babies, just as it has done for thousands of years. So, while doing your best to nourish and care for your body, have faith in it and its ability to produce a perfect baby.

Coping in the Early Days –
From Birth to Three Months

It's a wonderful moment when you wave goodbye to the nurses, usually within 24-48 hours of the birth, and take your baby home. But it's also daunting when you suddenly find that the responsibility for the welfare of this demanding and probably unpredictable small person now rests entirely with you. Added to this, you probably still feel tired and perhaps physically battered from the birth. Your hormones are in a state of transition, changing from a pregnant to a non-pregnant state and adjusting to breastfeeding.

Do not be surprised, therefore, if you feel fragile and weepy, just when everyone expects you to be feeling thrilled with your baby and on top of the world. This will come, but your body needs time to recover

and adapt. Emotionally, too, you need time to think over and relive the birth, and adjust to your new role. Giving birth is a tumultuous experience and both you and your partner need to be able to 'talk it out' during these early post-birth days. So do not set yourself any target just yet except that of gradually getting back your strength and helping your baby to settle into a harmonious routine. It's worth knowing, too, that it takes about six weeks for the milk supply to become firmly established. Once you have been feeding successfully for this length of time, it takes a very great deal to upset things. But until then, this is another reason for making an extra effort to look after yourself by avoiding unnecessary stresses and strains and taking care not to get too tired. In this context, it's worth remembering that some cultures, for instance the Vietnamese, expect the mother to remain in seclusion for the first month after birth, which I think is a good idea. I think we in the West could learn something from these cultures; we try to be "superwoman" and feel slightly guilty if we're not "back to normal" within a few days of the birth. I certainly felt emotionally fragile and vulnerable for at least a month after my babies were born.

Being Flexible

Babies aren't born with an instinctive knowledge of the difference between night and day, and few that I have met have sleeping and eating habits which conform in any way to the idea of "four-hourly feeds" and the neat little timetables given in old-fashioned baby books. Most new mothers are surprised and puzzled by the frequency with which their baby cries and wants to be picked up and fed: quite different from the mental picture they may have of a baby lying serenely asleep in her crib!

The first few weeks can therefore be somewhat chaotic, and in my opinion you will weather them best – and get the most enjoyment from your baby – if you can adopt a very flexible attitude. Accept that a pattern and routine will emerge, but that you and your baby need to grow into this together and that the process cannot be hurried. I realize that this attitude is easier for people like me who haven't much sense

of time, and rather enjoy doing things at odd hours, than for those who like a more organized, orderly existence. But trying to be too orderly and organized with a young baby is nerve-racking for all concerned. It is less harrowing if you can let the baby set the pace and fit your timetable into the baby's, rather than try to make your baby fit yours. Later, as you get used to your baby's pattern, you will find that you can manipulate it to some extent by either waking her for a feed or keeping her going for a bit longer before feeding.

Feeding Your New Baby

Milk is the only food your baby will need during the early days. You will need to decide whether you are going to breastfeed or bottlefeed.

Breast is Best

Health experts agree that breastmilk is the best food for your baby. The American Academy of Pediatrics says that, ideally, it's best for babies to be breastfed exclusively until they are at least six months old. Although formula milks are constantly being developed and improved, to make them more like breastmilk, they can never contain exactly the same cocktail of hormones, enzymes, and substances to help fight bacterial and viral infections. Breastmilk can also adjust if a baby is premature, alter as your baby grows and her needs change, and even dilute in hot weather to satisfy a baby's thirst. A bottle-feed cannot replace the closeness and skin contact your baby gets when feeding from you.

In addition, once breastfeeding is established, it's much easier and more practical than bottlefeeding. There's no sterilizing of equipment, no buying of milk powder, no making up of feeds, no heating up of milk during the small hours of the night, no chance of forgetting the baby's food if you go out for the day. Breastfeeding also helps your body to return to normal more quickly after the birth, because your uterus contracts when you breastfeed. It may also protect against cancer of the breast, ovaries, and cervix. In addition, if you breastfeed exclusively, it will reduce your chances of conceiving, though it cannot be relied on for contraception without another method.

If You Have to Bottlefeed...

Whether you breastfeed or bottlefeed, the most important thing is for you to have a relaxed, happy and rewarding feeding relationship with your baby. If you can't breastfeed, or for various reasons choose to bottlefeed, there are compensations. Babies often sleep better after a bottlefeed because formula milk forms curds in the stomach which makes them feel satisfied for longer. You may also feel less pressurized if other people can help with some of the feeds.

The First Breastfeed

The only preparation you need to make for breastfeeding while you are pregnant is to wash and dry your breasts normally when you have a bath or shower but don't use soap or shower gels which could wash away the natural lubricants. It's also good to get used to handling your breasts so that you don't feel awkward later on.

The baby's sucking reflex is at its strongest in the first few hours after birth, so when your baby is handed to you it is a good idea to put her straight to your breast. If, however, for some reason you feel you cannot do this (because you're too exhausted, too ill or just cannot make yourself), or if you try and the baby does not understand what to do, do not worry. Just try again quietly and gently a little later: perseverance and good support usually lead to success. I was worried when one of my daughters showed absolutely no interest in feeding just after she was born, but she had a feed a few hours later and subsequently proved to be the keenest breastfeeder of all.

Latching On

Do not wash your breasts before you feed. To put your baby to your breast, if you're sitting up (supported by pillows if necessary so that you feel relaxed and comfortable) rest her head on your forearm, making sure that you're holding her

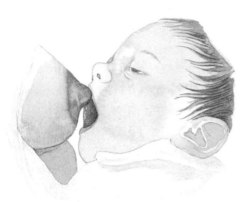

Brush baby's lips with your nipple until she opens her mouth really wide.

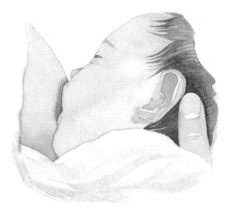

Bring her head towards your breast and ensure she takes the nipple and part of the breast.

with her body towards you so that she will not have to turn in order to reach your breast. Position her with her head tipped back slightly so that her chin is close to your breast and her lips are near your nipple: "chest to chest, chin to breast" is a good maxim. Brush her lips with your nipple until she opens her mouth. Wait until she opens her mouth really wide, almost as if she is going to yawn. This may take several minutes, so be patient. When it happens, quickly bring her head towards your breast so that she takes not just your nipple but also a good mouthful of breast as well. If she is latched on properly you will see her jawbone move as she sucks. If not, slide

your little finger into the corner of her mouth to break her suction and try again.

It is very important that your baby should have opened her mouth wide enough and be close enough to you to enable her to take a large mouthful of breast. This means that your nipple is protected from friction and will not get sore. Watch that your breast isn't covering your baby's nose and making breathing difficult: gently hold back your breast with your fingers if necessary to keep her nose free. Let your baby suck from one side until she comes off of her own accord, then offer the other breast only if necessary. After your baby has finished feeding, dry your breasts carefully. If you have problems with leaking, cover them with a disposable breast pad. Some people suggest putting on some nipple cream or using a spray but this is not advisable as it interferes with the delicate balance of natural secretions. Wash your nipples once a day without using soap, and keep them dry. Cotton bras can help also.

When the Milk Comes In

Giving short feeds as often as your baby will cooperate in the early days will give you both practice. During these early feeds, your baby is getting not milk but colostrum which helps her excrete the meconium from her bowel. Meconium is a sticky black waste product which builds up while your baby is in the womb. The actual milk comes in a few days after birth. This might be the second, third or fourth day. The milk usually comes in more quickly with second and subsequent babies, but the timing depends on how much sucking your baby has been able to do. The more you have been able to feed your baby, the more your breasts will have been stimulated, and the quicker the milk will come in, although until it does, the colostrum will supply all that your baby needs.

When the milk does come in you may well find that you are really "bursting" and the process is rather messy, although giving frequent brief feeds from the beginning will also help to minimize engorgement. Just keep on feeding your baby completely on demand and your supply will quickly adjust to her needs. If you find you have so much milk that it gushes out too quickly, making your baby splutter and choke, you can slow down the flow a little by holding your breast in your fingers, just above the areola, and pushing gently upwards.

In the early days you may find that milk leaks from your breasts between feeds; even hearing the cry of a baby can trigger the "let down reflex," which brings in the milk, and cause this to happen. A disposable breast pad inside your bra helps, as does wearing dark-colored tops which do not show up any wet patches too obviously. Don't let these inconveniences put you off. They all pass rapidly as you and your baby get used to breastfeeding. Before long, your breasts will shrink back to a much more normal size (even though they are producing large quantities of milk), they will not leak, and the whole process of breastfeeding will become smooth, easy and delightful.

Don't be in too much of a hurry to give supplementary bottles; many mothers do this because they doubt their own ability to produce enough milk. But your body responds to the baby's demand, so if you start to give bottles, the baby takes less milk from you, you produce less so you have to give more bottles and so it goes on. If you really want to breastfeed, just persevere, feed your baby on demand, and trust yourself and nature.

Expressing Milk

If your breasts become very full, they may get so firm that the baby has trouble taking your nipple. If you are engorged, expressing some milk first may make it easier for the baby to latch on. It's also useful to be able to express milk if your baby is born prematurely, so that she can be fed on your milk and, later, so that you can leave milk for her if you have to go out.

To express milk, hold your breast in one hand and use the other to stroke downwards towards the areola. Do this a number of times, to get the milk moving in the ducts. Then support your breast in the palm of your hand, with your thumb about halfway up your breast. Run your thumb down your breast towards the areola, pressing as you do so. Do it gently; don't bruise the tissue. The milk will spurt out of the nipple. If you're doing this simply to rid yourself of excess milk, you can do it over a washbasin. If your milk is being saved, to feed your baby, or for the hospital milk bank, then you will need to catch the milk in a sterilized jug or plastic container, cover and refrigerate immediately. You will never completely empty your breasts because, as they're stimulated, they make more milk; but you need to stop when the milk is only coming out in drops instead of spurts. If you have to express milk regularly, an electric breast pump is helpful. Manual breast pumps are much cheaper, though not quite as easy to use as the electric ones.

Breastfeeding Problems

Most mothers experience a few seconds of discomfort as the baby grasps the breast. After that it passes: it does not last for the whole feed. This sensation is caused by the rush of milk forcing the ducts open. It only happens during the first two or three weeks, and in fact the baby's sucking will help it to pass.

This kind of discomfort is different from the sort which lasts throughout the feed and indicates damage or stress to the surface of the nipple, thought to be caused by faulty positioning of the baby during feeding. This can be very painful, but can heal quickly. Calendula ointment, which you can get at health stores, is a natural and wonderfully soothing and healing ointment. You can also get excellent free advice from the groups listed under Useful Addresses (p. 151). If you have any problem with breastfeeding, ask for help early, from your midwife, physician, from another mother, or one of the groups mentioned.

Winding your Baby

After your baby has finished feeding, hold her up against your shoulder and gently rub or pat her back until she "burps." Make sure that she is straight; if she is curled up, her stomach will be squashed and the wind will not be able to come up. Some babies do not swallow much air as they feed, and not all babies need to burp at every feed, so don't worry if nothing happens. Don't worry either, by the way, if your baby brings up some milk after feeds. This is quite normal and just means she has had more than enough. The only kind of vomiting you need to take notice of, and report to your doctor immediately, is projectile vomiting, when the baby vomits with such force that the vomit shoots across the room. This may indicate a fault in the baby's stomach muscles which can be completely cured by a small operation.

Bottlefeeding

Unless for some reason you are unable to breastfeed, or really loathe the idea of breastfeeding, I think that it's a pity to start bottlefeeding until you have given breastfeeding a really good try. In this case, it's worth remembering that it can take up to six weeks or so to establish breastfeeding, not just ten days or two weeks, which is what some mothers seem to assume. So do not be in too much of a hurry to give up; do give yourself and your baby time to learn the art. Having tried, there is no reason to feel guilty if you are unable to breastfeed or choose to bottlefeed. It can be a satisfying experience.

For bottlefeeding, you will need six feeding bottles and teats: wide-necked bottles are easier to fill but may cost a bit more. Warm milk provides a perfect environment for bacteria; in addition, even the best formula milk does not contain the antibodies and natural immunity which passes from mother to baby in breastmilk. So you have to be scrupulous about hygiene when making up feeds, and the feeding bottles and all the equipment you use for measuring and mixing have to be thoroughly washed and sterilized after every use. To do this, you can use cold water with sterilizing tablets or liquid, which is the cheapest option; or buy an electric steam sterilizer which is convenient and uses no chemicals, or a microwave sterilizer which is compact.

It's important to buy a formula milk which has been specially designed for babies so that it is as much like human milk as possible. Don't be tempted to use ordinary cow's milk or evaporated milk which are not right for your baby's delicate digestion and could put too much strain on her kidneys. When deciding which type of milk to use, check that it is fortified with the vitamins your baby needs (and which she gets automatically from breastmilk). Also read the making-up instructions to see how easy it is to use.

Soy Formulas

If you are vegan you may wonder about the advisability of using soy baby milks since some concern has been expressed regarding their safety. This is because soy beans contain compounds called isoflavins. The isoflavins are also known as phytoestrogens and they behave like estrogen, the natural female hormone. Although the isoflavins are very weak (with 1:1,000 to 1:100,000 the potency of estrogen) they occur in very high concentrations so people eating soy products take in much higher levels of isoflavins than estrogen. So, do isoflavins have any ill-effects on humans in general and babies in particular?

In adults, rather than increasing estrogenic activity, isoflavins actually normalize estrogen levels. So women (such as the Japanese) who include soy products and soy milk in their diets have lower levels of estrogen in their bloodstream and thus a reduced risk of breast cancer. Conversely, isoflavins will raise the estrogen level in women who have abnormally low levels of estrogen in their blood. This raises the issue of what effects isoflavins may have on newborn babies and this is unknown and difficult to judge.

However the consensus of opinion amongst those who have studied this question carefully is that in assessing the possible dangers of using soy milk we need to look at what has happened to all those babies who have been raised on soy milk over the last 20 years. There has not been one human study demonstrating adverse effects (apart from allergic reactions) and there have been literally hundreds of studies demonstrating the positive effects of soy generally.

It's also worth remembering that cow's milk is itself loaded with estrogens and that these are not mild ones, derived from plants, but potent estrogens from another mammal which may well have some significant effects that have not yet been fully recognized, such as precocious puberty. On the evidence available, it seems that soy milk is a safe food both for babies and adults.

The Soy Milk Information Bureau states:

> Soy formulas are safe for use in babies under one year but they are not the first choice of baby milk and should only be used with good reason after medical and dietetic consultation. In all cases there should be a proven need for a non-dairy baby milk. When a soy-based product is required soy formulas rather than conventional soy milks should be used at least until the child is two years and may be used up to five years.

Making up formula varies slightly from brand to brand, so read the label. In general, the way to make up feeds is as follows. Wash your hands and boil enough water for the number of bottles you intend to make. Empty the kettle and put in fresh water – do not use water which has been boiled before, as the concentration of minerals could be too high. Put the correct amount into each feeding bottle, using the measure on the side, and let the water cool. (This is quicker than leaving it to cool in the kettle.) Measure the formula using the scoop provided. Don't pack it down, as too much powder can be harmful. Level it off with the back of a knife. Add the powder to the bottle, screw on the cap and shake well. Store the bottles in the fridge, and throw away any that are unused after 24 hours.

Some babies like their formula straight from the fridge. Others prefer the bottle warmed in a bottle warmer or jug of hot water. To give a bottlefeed, cradle your baby in the crook of your arm so that she is cosy and close to you. When practical, open your shirt so that she can feel your warm skin. Gently touch the baby's cheek nearest to you; as she turns towards you, pop the teat into her mouth. Make sure you tilt the bottle well so that the milk fills the teat-end of the bottle and no air can get in, which could give her colic. (Anti-colic teats are available from the pharmacist.) Pull on the bottle a little as your baby sucks, to keep up the suction. After your baby has finished the feed, "burp" her (see p. 32).

Coping during the Day

In these early days your baby will be happiest and you will probably cope best if you pick her up when she cries and offer a feed. Although this is the most natural thing to do, for some reason most people – and I was the same myself – have the feeling that their baby ought to sleep for longer and conform roughly to the ideal of four-hourly feeds, each followed by a peaceful sleep! Then there are plenty of well-meaning people only too ready to tell you that you're spoiling your baby by picking her up, that your baby is only crying because "she wants you to pick her up," and that "the baby needs to exercise her lungs by crying." But you cannot "spoil" such a tiny baby, and her lungs do not need any exercise other than that which she gets every time she breathes. And yes, your baby probably is crying because she wants you to pick her up. But if you think about it, that, too, is natural, considering how close your baby has been to you for nine months. The physical closeness between you needs to continue, easing away very gently and gradually over the weeks and months.

Feeding on Demand

When your baby cries, assume that she wants feeding, and put her to your breast, even if the last feed was as recent as half an hour ago. This frequent feeding will, as I have already said, stimulate your breasts to produce more milk, thus increasing your supply. It's because breastfeeding depends on this supply-and-demand system that breastmilk, though a perfect food, does not sustain your baby for as long as formula milk. Breastfed babies need feeding more often than those who are on formula, which I see as nature's way of ensuring that the transition from womb to independence should be a very gradual one. If you get a situation where it is essential for your baby to sleep for a period of three or four hours, for your own sanity, the preservation of your marriage, or some other reason, giving your baby about $^1/_4$ cup of formula milk from a bottle (if she will take a bottle) will probably ensure this. It can also be a good idea to give your baby an occasional bottle of, say, boiled, cooled water, to get her used to taking a bottle. But if you're serious about breastfeeding, this is best kept as a last resort, rather than becoming a habit.

Of course, babies do cry for reasons other than wanting to be cuddled and fed, and as the days go by you will get to understand what the various cries mean and when, for instance, your baby is crying with irritable exhaustion just prior to falling asleep. But at this stage, when your baby is so tiny and you are trying to establish the feeding, I think it is best to try a cuddle and a feed first, before she gets so upset that she finds it impossible to feed. Remember that you can't overfeed a breastfed baby and in many parts of the world feeding continues virtually all the time, with the contented baby carried in a sling at her mother's breast, able to have a little suck whenever she feels the need. It may well be the comfort of sucking, and the knowledge of your closeness, which your baby needs, rather than food. If you have a very "cuddly" baby, you might find it helpful to use a sling.

Comforting your Baby

If you feel that your baby is overly restless, check that she is the right temperature. Being small, babies lose and gain heat quickly and their hands are not always a good guide to their body temperature. So make sure that your baby is cosily wrapped up and keep the room comfortably warm. On the other hand, your baby can get overheated in a warm room if you pile on too many blankets, so you need to be vigilant to get it just right. Don't put her out in the baby carriage for long periods of time. A tiny baby's need for fresh air is greatly overstated; it is much more important to see that she is warm enough, and a normal airy room can supply all the "fresh air" she needs.

Something else which can have a soothing effect if your baby is restless is to wrap a shawl firmly around her, then tuck in the covers firmly and cosily when you put her down in the crib. This gives her the feeling of being securely held. When your baby no longer needs to be so firmly tucked up, she will let you know by wriggling and kicking off the covers.

If you have a very "sucky" baby and find the almost constant feeding too much to cope with, you might consider giving your baby a pacifier. Most new parents don't give their baby a pacifier when it would be very helpful, for example for colic or during fretful evenings, because they are terrified that she will become addicted and they will never be able to get the pacifier away. But your baby will give up the pacifier of her own accord between three and five months old, when she is less desperate for comfort-sucking. We gave our eldest child a pacifier and it was such a comfort to all concerned! She gave it up spontaneously at four and a half months when her first tooth was coming through. A pacifier can be a great comfort to mother and baby alike, and I certainly recommend them as long as they're not used so excessively that they prevent the baby from getting all the physical comfort and cuddles she needs, and the frequent feeds which help to establish breastfeeding in the early days.

If you do use a pacifier, keep it scrupulously clean by placing it in a sterilizer when your baby is not using it. Never put any form of sweetener on the pacifier and do not give your baby a pacifier containing fruit juice or other liquid. These will interfere with her demand for breastmilk and may have a detrimental effect on her teeth.

Don't feel that you have to give your baby a bath every day. A daily bath is fine if you have the time and if your baby likes it. But many newborn babies dislike their bath, and this, combined with a new mother's natural apprehension and awkwardness, can make the bath a worrying time for both. Your baby will be fine as long as she is "topped-and-tailed."

Lively Babies

Some babies just seem to be born lively and if you happen to have one of these you will not get much peace. She certainly will not sleep for as long as other babies and she will want to see what is going on.

The way to cope with a baby like this is to let her be wherever you are, in the midst of the household clamor. Put your baby where she can see you, in one of those little rocking cradle chairs, baby car seat or convertible reclining chair, or prop her up in her crib or in a chair. Make sure that she is firmly supported with cushions and cannot slip. Talk to your baby often – the sound of your voice will be reassuring – and make sure there is always plenty for her to look at. Colored mobiles are a good idea and are quite inexpensive to make, using colored cardboard cut into shapes or small colorful objects strung up from a hook in the ceiling. An alternative is to stretch a piece of rope across the baby's carriage and peg or tie on to it different items such as brightly colored tissue paper, a string of bells, a piece of bright ribbon. Change the objects often to keep the baby's interest. Babies also like looking at colored birthday cards or pictures pushed down the sides of the crib and baby carriage. A musical box is often a great success with tiny babies. You could also buy a recording of simulated womb noises which has a calming effect on a restless baby: I believe a recording of an automatic washing machine, with its whirls and gurgles, has a similar effect; or, easier still, simply put the baby near the washing machine!

However hard you try you will probably get one of those days when your baby never seems to stop demanding and you feel at your wits' end. This is the time when it's so marvelous if you have a kind neighbor who understands this desperate feeling and will take your baby, immediately, for half an hour to give you a breather. But if you haven't such a neighbor, remember that ten minutes of crying never hurt any baby. Put her out of earshot, make yourself a drink, and set the timer for ten minutes. Then relax. You'll be surprised how different you feel when the timer goes and you return to your baby.

When you're struggling with a difficult baby who is lively, never sleeps, and cries easily with frustration or boredom, it's sometimes helpful to remember that all the characteristics you find such hard work have a flip side: aggression = drive; obstinacy = perseverance; liveliness = interest in life, and so on. Babies who are very hard work become children who never cease to amaze and delight you. It's tempting to think "oh for a dim baby who sleeps:" but is that what you really want?

Coping during the Evening

One of the most difficult times with a young baby is in the evening when many seem to have a fretful period just when you are tired and longing to have an hour or so to yourself. This, in my opinion, is where demand-feeding is such a help.

The way I coped with this difficult time, which I had with all three of my daughters, was to get in a good supply of interesting books and magazines, make myself a soothing drink, sit in a comfortable chair with my feet up, and let the baby feed while I relaxed.

It is a demanding stage and if you adopt my policy it does mean that your evenings are a write-off and it's useless to plan any social life, so you'll need the understanding and support of the rest of the family. But though it seems hard to believe at the time, this stage passes very quickly – within a few weeks – and you will probably look back on it with some nostalgia in the future.

You may well feel that there is not much milk left at the end of the day but, as I have explained, your baby's sucking action will stimulate the milk so the more she sucks, the more there will be. If, on the other hand, you think your baby is wanting to suck for comfort, rather than for food, you might well find that a pacifier could be the answer. I know it's not aesthetically pleasing, but it could make all the difference to your evenings. If you think your baby is wanting to suck because she is hungry, and that the problem is that you're short of milk in the evenings, it is better to try to increase your own supply, if you wish to continue with breastfeeding, rather than to start giving supplementary feeds from a bottle.

Increasing Your Supply of Milk

● Feed your baby more often
● Check your baby's position to make sure she's stimulating your breasts and

is able to get all your milk

- Let her finish at one breast, then offer the other
- Check that you are eating and drinking enough; this is not the time to worry about dieting or losing weight – that will happen naturally as the weeks go by
- Make sure you are getting as much rest as you can; accept all offers of help
- Remember that it takes several days to increase your milk supply (you won't see much change in less than 48 hours), so keep on trying for at least two weeks before you judge the results

Quick Nutritious Snacks for Breastfeeding Moms

During breastfeeding your need for extra nutrients continues. Boosting normal meals with one or two nutritious snacks during the day will ensure that you (and your baby) are well-nourished. At first it's hard even to find time to make breakfast or lunch for yourself so having several good-quality snacks could be more practical. Choose from the Five-Star Foods (p. 19) as often as you can. Here are some suggestions:

- A handful of mixed nuts and seeds with dried fruit
- A bowl of Very Quick Lentil Soup (p. 101) with whole wheat bread
- Lentil dal with spiced rice
- Whole wheat peanut butter, tahini, hummus, or cheese sandwich with salad
- Hummus (p. 91), salad, and pita bread
- Tahini Dip (p. 90) or Hummus (p. 91)

with vegetables

- Banana shake: blend a banana in some milk or soy milk (B12- and calcium-fortified) with 2 teaspoons blackstrap molasses and $1/2$ cup ground almonds
- A bowl of creamy oatmeal (made with half water, half milk or soy milk) topped with slivered almonds or ground hazelnuts
- Quick brown rice salad: mix chopped red or green bell pepper, onion, tomato with cooked brown rice and some toasted pumpkin or sesame seeds; serve sprinkled with Gomasio (p. 89)
- Red Kidney Bean and Avocado Salad (p. 99) with whole wheat or pita bread
- Felafel (p. 126) with salad and Tahini Dressing (p. 90) in pita bread
- Any of the iron-rich snacks on pp. 143 and 147
- Nourishing Fruit Cake (p. 139), Parkin (p. 140), Fruit and Nut Bars (p. 141), or Molasses Oat Bars (p. 137)
- Bought vegeburger or Spicy Bean-burger (p. 127) in a whole wheat bun with Tahini Dressing (p. 90)

Evening Colic

In the evening very many babies seem to have a restless, fretful period, when they cry more than usual, and often parents think that the reason for this is 'colic'. When a baby has colic (which often does not start until she is about a month old), she appears to be in real pain, drawing her knees up to her stomach, crying and sobbing uncontrollably. Nothing seems to comfort her for any length of time; doctors do not know the cause of the problem and there seems to be little that they can do to help.

Gripe water is sometimes helpful or you can make a dill water by steeping a teaspoonful of lightly crushed dill seeds in a couple of tablespoons of boiling water, cooling and straining. A pacifier can also be helpful. Warmth, from a well-wrapped hot water bottle, put near (but not on top of) the baby's tummy, can also help. And some mothers find merbentyl, from the doctor, works for true colic. But one of the troubles with real colic is that there seems to be so little you can do. You keep trying things, and these seem to work for a short time, then the screaming and drawing-up of the legs starts again and you're at a loss as to what to do.

If your baby really has got colic, it is not because of something you're doing wrong. It's just one of those inexplicable things, and you will have to face the fact that you're going to have very difficult evenings for a few weeks, giving her what comfort and reassurance you can. This is extremely taxing and demanding, and it will help if you and your partner can take turns to cope alternately with your baby throughout the evening. The only really comforting thing I can say is that colic rarely lasts for more than eight weeks and invariably stops, usually quite suddenly, by the time the baby is three to four months old.

Coping at Night

When you put your baby down for the night, it's a good idea to try and create a different atmosphere from day-time sleeps. Put your baby in her crib in the bedroom; make sure that the room is warm and dark, with perhaps just a low light, so that you do not have to switch on more light and risk waking her when you go to bed yourself or when you're dealing with night feeds.

Making Night Feeds Easy

Unless you are very lucky, once you do finally get to sleep you will probably be awakened at least once during the night. However, breastfeeding does make the night-time feeds relatively easy to cope with, and if you can manage to feed the baby while she is still sleepy the chances are that you will both fall asleep again very quickly. So don't let your baby cry for any length of time; have her near you, if possible right by your bed so that you only have to reach over and pick her up. You can then feed her easily, almost in your sleep, and both go back to sleep again quickly.

Unless you have a very fussy baby, most experienced mothers agree that it is much better not to try and change a diaper in the night unless it is obviously causing discomfort. If you feed quickly and then put your baby straight back into the crib without messing about with creams and diapers, you will both have a better chance of getting back to sleep again.

If you go along with your baby's needs for night feeds, you will find that, just like the day, a pattern gradually emerges. The time between feeds will grow longer. You may find that you can manipulate the time of the night feeds by waking your baby for a feed just before you go to sleep, so that then, with any luck, you can get an unbroken sleep during the early part of the night.

Thinking Ahead

A little forethought can make all the difference to how you feel and how you cope in the early days after the birth. If this is your first baby you will probably have little idea how dramatically her arrival will affect you, your partner and your home. At first, the needs of your baby will fully occupy you, to the exclusion of almost everything else. If your baby is anything like the majority, you will also have to put up with many interruptions during the night. And you will be coping with all this, having been through the incredibly intense experience of childbirth, with its enormous demands on you, physically, mentally, and emotionally.

For all these reasons, it's worth organizing things so that your life is as easy as possible during the first six weeks or so after the birth. Accept all offers of help with housework, washing, and shopping. Having a relative or friend to stay, or to pop in for a few hours each day for a week or so after the birth, to deal with the cleaning, washing, and cooking, can make such a difference. Whether or not this is possible, it's worth looking at your home from the point of view of easy cleaning. Remove any unnecessary dust traps like ornaments, for instance, and get an extension cord for the vacuum cleaner so that you can use it in several rooms without having to unplug it.

It is not being overly cautious to make a rough meal plan now, perhaps along the lines of the one on pp. 17-19, getting the appropriate dishes safely stashed away in the freezer.

In fact the more complete meals you can get into the freezer before your baby is born, the better. All dishes marked (*) in this book freeze well. In addition, it's helpful to have some of the following "freezer basics" for making vegetarian meals quickly and easily:

Tomato sauce
Useful for topping pizzas, serving with pasta, polenta, and other dishes. Make a large quantity, using the recipe on p. 92, and freeze in suitable 1-cup containers.

Whole wheat pie shells
Warm these through while you make an easy filling mixture, and put the two together for a quick and satisfying meal. They're not difficult to make – see p. 129. Freeze them until solid, then remove from their pie pans and pack carefully for freezing.

Pizza dough

Make a batch of this (see p. 132) and freeze it in 4 separate portions. Then simply defrost a portion as necessary, roll it out thinly, top with tomato sauce if you have it, and some or all of the following: sliced onions, tomatoes, bell peppers, canned or frozen corn, olives, and cheese if you like it. Bake for 15 minutes at 400°F for a wonderful, easy homemade pizza which will fill the house with welcoming smells.

A variety of breads

Stock up on a few of your favorite types of bread; basic whole wheat or a batch of your own whole wheat Molasses Bread (p. 138); whole wheat pita breads, and burger buns for quick snacks; focaccia or multigrain for a change; some Indian breads if you like them.

Prepared dishes

The most useful dishes to make for the freezer are those which are complete in themselves (or with a sauce that you freeze with them) and that need only a simple vegetable or salad to accompany them – casserole dishes, homemade pizzas or pies, polenta ready for broiling or frying. Spiced rice dishes and dals will freeze for at least 4-6 weeks without developing 'off' flavors. Both Felafel (p. 126) and Spicy Beanburgers (p. 127) can be used from frozen to make quick lunches and snacks.

Stocking the Shelves

In addition to stocking the freezer, as your pregnancy draws to a close, you'll want to make sure that your cupboard and refrigerator are well stocked with some of the basics needed for making quick meals.

Grains

Long-grain and basmati brown rice, and short-grain arborio for risottos. Rolled oats, bulgur, buckwheat groats if you like them; also couscous. Not really a grain, but nutritious and nice for a treat is wild rice.

Flours

Whole wheat, for making pastry and bread; a brown bread flour for making pizza. Polenta – cornmeal – is useful.

Pasta

A supply of your favorites. My own include penne, rigatoni, fusilli, and tagliatelle.

Dried beans and lentils

Split red lentils, whole brown or Puy lentils, split yellow peas and butter beans – and chick peas and red kidney beans if you've got the patience to cook them.

Cans

Canned chick peas and red kidney beans; tomatoes in juice; corn kernels for salads and pizza toppings (corn is quite a useful source of nutrients, including iron and B vitamins).

Nuts and seeds

Powerhouses of concentrated nutrients; use in small quantities and keep fresh by storing in the freezer or fridge. Most useful are almonds, pistachios (especially rich in iron), cashews; pumpkin, sunflower, and sesame seeds. Get the unroasted, dull browny-gray sesame seeds (not the white ones which have been hulled in brine or with chemicals). A jar – or more – of pale tahini and also peanut butter without added salt, sugar or palm oil. A packet of unsweetened shredded coconut .

Fresh soy products

A packet or two of firm tofu, which will keep in the fridge; useful for Chinese stir-fries and Tofu Satay (pp. 123-4); soft tofu for creamy Apricot or Mango Fool (p. 149). It's also worth stocking up on your favorite types of soy milk, yogurt, and cream if you like these.

Oils and fats

Butter or good-quality pure vegetable margarine; olive oil; peanut or soybean oil for frying and some baking.

Flavorings

Red wine vinegar, black olives, green olives, sea salt, garlic, hot chili sauce, and cheap sherry for Chinese stir-fries. Molasses and nutritional yeast flakes for their nutrient value. Some dried yeast if you want to make bread or pizzas. A packet of kombu seaweed for flavoring and arame for eastern-style salads: both are rich in minerals. A packet of dried porcini mushrooms for making a special risotto – optional but a nice treat. Tub of dry whole wheat crumbs for coating homemade burgers.

Spices

Bay leaves, cardamom pods, cayenne or chili powder, dried chilies, powdered cinnamon, whole and ground coriander seeds, whole and ground cumin seeds, fenugreek, ground ginger, ground turmeric.

TWO WEEKS' EASY MENUS FOR THE EARLY DAYS AFTER YOUR BABY'S BIRTH
(Dishes marked * are suitable for freezing)

	LUNCH	DINNER
DAY 1	Felafel* (p. 126) in pita bread with salad Fresh fruit or vegetable juice and/or fresh fruit	Spiced Vegetable Pilau* (p. 121) with tomato and onion salad and Indian bread Fruit and yogurt
DAY 2	Leftover Spiced Vegetable Pilau, with chutney, tomato and watercress or brown rice salad Fresh juices and/or fruit	Rigatoni with Mediterranean Sauce* (p. 135) with mixed salad Nectarines
DAY 3	Very Quick Lentil Soup* (p. 101) with bread and crudités Fresh juices and/or fruit	Broccoli and Corn Pie* (p. 130) with steamed carrots or mixed salad and mashed potatoes Ripe pears
DAY 4	Leftover Broccoli and Corn Pie and/or baked potato with Hummus* (p. 91) and mixed salad Fresh juices and/or fruit	Roasted Vegetables with Oven-Baked Rice (p. 114) with green salad Baked Peaches (p. 145)
DAY 5	Leftover Roasted Vegetables with Oven-Baked Rice made into a rice salad or Chick Pea, Tomato, and Green Bell Pepper Salad (p. 97) with pita bread Fresh juices and/or fruit	Parsley and Onion Polenta* (p. 116) with Tomato Sauce* (p.92) and steamed broccoli and potatoes Ripe cherries
DAY 6	Parsley and Onion Polenta* (p. 116) and mixed salad with Non-Egg Mayonnaise (p. 89) or Avocado Salad Sandwiches (p. 107) Fresh juices and/or fruit	Mediterranean Butter Bean Casserole* (p. 110) with crusty whole wheat bread Exotic Fruit Salad (p. 148)
DAY 7	Leftover Mediterranean Butter Bean Casserole in pita bread Fresh juices and/or fruit	Bulgur with Broiled Vegetables (p. 112) Fresh dates stuffed with whole Brazil nuts or cream cheese
DAY 8	Bruschetta with Hummus, Tomato, and Olives (p. 108) Fresh juices and/or fruit	Creamy Cashew Nut Korma* (p. 120) with brown rice and Indian Carrot Salad (p. 95) Grapes
DAY 9	Leftover Cashew Nut Korma with Indian bread or Avocado and Alfalfa in a Burger Bun (p.106) Fresh juices and/or fruit	Tagliatelle with Broccoli Cream Sauce* (p. 134) and mixed salad Raspberries

	LUNCH	DINNER
DAY 10	Felafel* (p.126) and Salad or Eggplant, Chili, and Tahini (p. 106) in whole wheat pita bread Fresh juices and/or fruit	Tomato and Onion Pizza* (p. 133) with green salad Apples and Raisins (p. 146)
DAY 11	Leftover Tomato and Onion Pizza and/or baked potato with garlic butter and mixed salad Fresh juices and/or fruit	Spinach Dal* (p. 119) with tomato salad and Indian bread Mango Fool (p. 149) or fresh fruit
DAY 12	Spicy Beanburger* (p. 127) in a whole wheat bun Fresh juices and/or fruit	Leek and Potato Pie* (p. 131) and mashed potatoes, mixed salad or steamed vegetables Bananas with Ginger (p. 150)
DAY 13	Leftover Leek and Potato Pie with mixed salad and/or baked potato with Tahini Dip (p. 90) or Hummus (p. 91) Fresh juices and/or fruit	Lentil and Broccoli Gratin* (p. 118) with baked or mashed potatoes and steamed carrots Baked Apples with Raisins (p. 145) or Baked Bananas (p. 146)
DAY 14	Leftover Lentil and Broccoli Gratin with chutney and green salad or Greek Split Pea Soup* (p. 102) with whole wheat bun Fresh juices and/or fruit	Tofu Satay (p. 124) and Eastern-Style Salad with Arame (p. 95) Litchi and Kiwi Fruit Salad (p. 148)

Notes on Menus

- For Breakfast Ideas, see p. 19.
- Some people go off spicy food while pregnant and in the early days after the birth. If this applies to you, you may wish to go easy on the spices in the Indian and Chinese dishes or simply replace them with other legume or grain dishes. Other people won't experience any problems and may even feel particularly keen on such dishes – it's best to follow your own instincts. While breastfeeding, watch out for any adverse reaction from your baby when you eat spicy food, especially dishes containing chili and garlic. Again, if these seem to be associated with your baby getting colic or indigestion, you may be better off replacing them with other dishes.
- It is helpful to save a portion of the evening meal for your lunch the following day, either to reheat or to eat cold.
- It is assumed that you will take about 3 cups of milk or soy milk during the day, in drinks, snacks, on breakfast cereals, and in main dishes where applicable.
- Desserts are optional, but the ones I've given are relatively simple. Yogurt or soy yogurt could be included in many of them as a good way of consuming extra milk.

Your Baby – From Three to Six Months

Gradually you'll find the chaos and unpredictability of the early baby days pass; you and your baby will evolve a harmonious routine, and she will respond increasingly to you and begin to take a lively interest in the world around her. Babies begin to be fun at around this age and there are various things you can do to entertain your baby and help her to develop mentally. Research has shown that the more time you spend playing with and talking to your baby, the more quickly she will develop and the more intelligent she is likely to be. Looking after a baby is certainly a great deal more interesting, rewarding and enjoyable if you have some ideas for stimulating and playing with her.

Entertaining Your Baby

Your baby will still enjoy all the things described on p. 37: colored pictures on the walls beside the crib or pushed down the sides of the crib and baby carriage (well secured, or she will grab and eat them as she gets older); colored mobiles to look at; a musical box to listen to. In addition, when your baby is around two to three months old, she will enjoy being able to reach out and touch a fluffy ball or rattle suspended from the carriage hood or from a piece of cane lashed across the crib. Those suction rattles which you can buy to stick to the high chair or the wall beside the crib are also great fun for your baby, as is a 'mobile gym', which consists of various toys for her to push and pull, mounted on a plastic bar that you tie across the crib.

From about three months babies begin to enjoy exploring things with their hands. They like to touch a rattle, a string of wooden beads or soft toys, or a bunch of keys. Give your baby plenty of different objects to handle and study, varying the shapes and textures: a piece of soft material, a small furry toy, some crackly shiny paper rolled into a ball, tissue paper to handle and tear, small empty cardboard boxes and plastic bottles, pieces of sponge, empty egg boxes, rattles made by putting some dried beans or lentils into a plastic container with a firmly secured lid. Again, watch for eating; the baby son of a friend of mine used to eat his older sisters' comics and they would come out in his diaper still readable! And I have vivid memories of one of my babies eating handfuls of small pebbles on the beach. I did not realize she had actually swallowed any until I saw what came through in her diaper!

A baby this age will also enjoy playing with your kitchen utensils; a plastic bowl is fun to fill with ping pong balls and, a little later on, saucepans are great to bang with a wooden spoon.

From the age of about three months, as soon as she can hold her head unsupported, your baby can be put into a baby bouncer. This is a little fabric harness attached to a piece of springy rubber which fastens to a hook in the ceiling or to a clip over the door frame. As your baby puts a toe on the ground, she will bounce. She will get a great deal of pleasure from bouncing several times a day – and you will be free for a few minutes to get on with something nearby.

Interacting with Your Baby

If yours is a lively baby, you'll be used to having her beside you in her little rocking chair or car seat. All babies will now need this opportunity and will watch happily as you go about your tasks.

Continue to talk to your baby frequently and repeat the sounds which she makes to you. She will love the rhythm of songs and rhymes and will soon respond to games of "peekaboo," and action rhymes, such as "pat-a-cake," "this little piggy went to market" and "round and round the garden." Nursery rhyme books and tapes are useful for jogging rusty memories. Your baby will also love brightly colored picture books.

During this period (between three and six months) your baby will learn to roll over; to sit unsupported for a few seconds and to prepare to crawl; she will love to pull herself up on your knee and bounce about, supported by your body and reassured by your closeness. You can encourage your baby's physical development by letting her lie on a rug in a warm room or sunny garden with the minimum of clothing, protected as necessary by sunblock.

Although they're demanding, babies

at this stage can be enormously rewarding and fun. The more you cuddle, talk to, and play with your baby, the more you will get out of the relationship, and the quicker she will develop. Giving your baby this close attention is not "spoiling;" it is helping her to develop as fully as possible.

Some mothers seem to enjoy all this naturally; others find themselves distraught with boredom and frustration, resenting and begrudging every demand. Because they're emotionally drained by the effort of meeting their baby's increasing needs, they hold back, trying to keep something in reserve. The baby soon senses this and becomes more demanding as a result. So a vicious circle begins.

If this is a problem for you, I can only say that, paradoxically, the more quickly and fully you meet your baby's demands, the more contented and "easy" she will be and the more chance you'll both have of being reasonably happy. I strongly advise this course of action, though you may receive advice to the contrary, such as "you'll spoil the baby," or "the baby mustn't be taught to think she can have everything she wants." I do not agree with these statements and in my experience the reverse is true, as I have explained above. The more certain your baby is of having her needs met, the less anxious and demanding she will become. She will learn from an early age to have a basic confidence in the goodness of life and the expectation that her emotional needs will be met. In any case, a baby of this age is far too young to be able to use her "power" over you in a calculating way; she is just aware of her needs – for food, comfort, stimulation, love – and that you are the person who will satisfy them.

Looking After Yourself

I personally found I coped best if I considered my baby to be my full-time job during the day, not planning to do anything else except absolutely essential shopping and cooking, and the minimum of necessary cleaning. Then I would look forward to an hour or so of my own in the evening when she was in bed. I certainly found it helpful to line up plenty of activities to keep her happy and amused during the day.

It can also be a very great help to get out and meet other mothers who are in a similar position. Such gatherings, whether sponsored and organized by a group or run on a more informal basis, provide social contact which can be such a morale-booster at this time. I certainly found this to be so, as it is comforting and therapeutic to be able to swap experiences and realize you're not alone in what you're going through. Teaming up with another mother so that you each take it in turns to look after both babies on a regular basis can also be most helpful. It's less emotionally draining to look after two babies for, say, a couple of hours, knowing that later you will get a couple of hours to yourself.

Going Back to Work

Going back to work doesn't have to mean the end of breastfeeding. At the very least you could fit in a cosy feed early in the morning before you leave, to bind you both together before the separation of the working day. Then when you return in the evening you can greet your baby with another feed, helping you to readjust to motherhood; and you can go on feeding your baby during the evening (and in the night as necessary), as much as you wish. Many working mothers find that their babies wake more for feeds during the night after they have returned to work. You can take your baby into bed with you and feed her while you are lying down. This is perfectly safe as long as neither partner has had a sedative or alcohol.

For daytime feeds you can express milk for your baby to have while you are away, or arrange for your baby to have formula milk or juice and food, or if you work close to home perhaps your baby could be brought to you for feeds, or you might try a combination of all of these possibilities. It will depend on the age of your baby and how far away you work as well as what feels right for you. Only you can decide. If you express milk while away from home, it must be kept cool, preferably in a fridge. Milk which you express at lunchtime could be used the next day. Breastmilk freezes well and will keep for three months, so you can build up a milk bank. Remember to sterilize all the equipment you use and label the milk with the date. Defrost the milk quickly by standing it in warm water just before you use it. Throw out any that is left over after the feed.

If your decision involves fewer feeds, give your body time to adjust so that your breasts don't feel uncomfortably full when you are at work. Decide which feeds you will be dropping and stop them, one by one, over a few weeks leading up to your return to work. Let your body adjust to one less feed before dropping another. Many women find themselves getting tearful during this weaning stage – another reason to take things slowly.

If your decision involves bottlefeeds, whether of formula or your own expressed milk, you will need to start getting your baby used to taking a feed from a bottle in good time. She may need several goes to get the hang of it and may take it better from someone else, as she associates you with breastmilk. Keep offering gently, without pressure, and she will probably accept. If she doesn't, she can be fed from a spoon during the day before four months and from a feeder cup after that.

Teething

Towards the end of this six-month period the first tooth or teeth may appear. The timing does vary a good deal, with some babies remaining toothless until around a year, so do not worry if your baby's half-birthday passes without any sign of a tooth. Babies often have some discomfort when cutting their teeth, more especially with the back teeth, which appear during their second year, than with the first front teeth. Nevertheless your baby may find it comforting to chew on a teething ring which should be kept sterilized when not in use.

Incidentally, you don't need to stop breastfeeding when your baby's teeth appear. Strangely enough, these do not hurt. This is because your baby's mouth is filled by your nipple and the areola around it, and so the jaws are open, not closed. Sometimes your baby may inadvertently bite at the end of a feed, after she has finished sucking and when she is just "playing" with your breast. Prevent this by removing the breast as soon as your baby has finished feeding; she will quickly learn not to bite.

Weaning Your Baby

Weaning, or getting your baby to switch from an all-milk diet to one that includes solid foods, is a process many mothers view with some apprehension. I felt that way myself; if anything it's worse for us vegetarian mothers, who may not know which vegetarian foods are suitable for a baby and may be further unsettled by anxious friends and relatives. However, the weaning process is really a very simple one, and most babies accomplish it amazingly smoothly. Parents can be reassured that a vegetarian diet can offer all the nourishment a baby needs for growth and development. This is how the weaning process might go:

When Your Baby is Four to Six Months Old

You can give your baby a little fresh, unsweetened fruit juice, diluted half-and-half with boiled, cooled water. Apple juice is the best choice because it is less likely to cause an allergic reaction than orange juice. Give this fruit juice, diluted with a little boiled, cooled water, initially from a teaspoon, in the middle of the morning or afternoon. As soon as your baby gets used to taking it in this way, try giving it from a normal cup (not a mug with a feeder lid). This is an excellent way of introducing your baby to a cup. Your baby will be able to drink from a feeder cup at about six months. It's a good idea for her to be able to use both a feeder cup and an ordinary cup. Apart from this juice, continue with breastfeeding or bottlefeeding in the normal way.

Breastmilk supplies all that your baby needs (including vitamin C) for the first six months of life. So if your baby is happy and thriving, there is no need to think about introducing any solids until she is six months old. If, however, after four months your baby does not seem fully satisfied with milk, you might try giving a first taste of food – but don't start before four months. (The danger of introducing solids early is that your baby's immature digestive system cannot readily cope with the food, and so the likelihood of an allergic reaction is increased.)

First Foods

The first spoonfuls are really just to get your baby used to the taste and feel of solid food. Do not think of them as a real source of nourishment at this stage. Your baby still needs milk feeds for that and also for the emotional satisfaction of sucking.

Half a teaspoonful of a fruit or vegetable puree (see pp. 52-3) is best for your baby's first taste of solid food. Traditionally cereals were always the first solid food given to babies. However, these are now advised against, as they can cause allergies if given too early.

Use a flat teaspoon and give the first taste at one of the main milk feeds corresponding to breakfast, lunch, or dinner, whichever is the most convenient for you. If you are planning to go back to work but want to continue breastfeeding, start giving the solids at lunchtime, for this will eventually become the first meal at which your baby gives up a breastfeed and just has solids.

Whether you give the first taste of solid food before or after the milk feed is up to you, or perhaps, more to the point, up to your baby! But generally speaking, it's better to give solids before the milk feed if you can so that, as you gradually increase the quantity of solids, your baby will be satisfied with these and forget about the milk feed. However, there is no point in trying to give solids if your baby is hungry, wanting comfort, and crying for a feed. Better to let her feed first and then give the taste of solids at the end.

Be prepared for the fact that your baby may well spit out your lovingly prepared offerings. Don't worry and don't take it personally. She is not depending on this food for nourishment at this stage. Try again another day, persisting gently; there is no hurry.

As your baby gets used to the flavor, you can gradually increase the quantity so that after a few weeks she is having perhaps two tablespoonfuls of food at a time. Increasing the quantity gradually also gives your baby's digestive system plenty of time to become used to coping with solid food.

Allergies

Many mothers worry about possible allergic reactions when they introduce their babies to new foods. Actually allergies are quite rare and where they do occur they are usually inherited, so you will know in advance if they are likely. Delaying the introduction of solid foods until your baby is at least four months old, or preferably six months, makes the risk of an allergic reaction less likely because her digestive system is more able to cope.

The most common foods to cause allergies are milk and dairy products, eggs, nuts, sugar, chocolate, oranges, wheat and

FOODS FOR WEANING AND HOW TO PREPARE THEM

FOOD	PREPARATION
Carrot	Scrape carrot and boil it in a little unsalted water until tender; puree with enough of the cooking water to get a soft consistency. Start by giving $1/2$ teaspoon before or after the midday or evening milk feed.
Rutabaga, parsnip	Make like carrot puree.
Applesauce	Use sweet apples only, not tart ones that require added sweetening. Peel, core, and slice apple; cook in 2-3 tablespoons water until tender; puree, adding a little extra boiled water if necessary to get a soft consistency.
Pear puree	Make like applesauce, using sweet pears.
Banana	Choose very ripe bananas. Peel. Remove the seeds with the point of a knife if you like. Mash flesh thoroughly with a fork, adding a little cooled boiled water if necessary to get a soft consistency.
Zucchini	Cut off the ends. Cut into small pieces, cook in a minimum of unsalted water until tender. Puree with enough cooking water to get a soft consistency.
Pumpkin, winter squash	Peel; remove the seeds. Cut the flesh into pieces and cook in a little boiling water until tender. Puree.
Tomato	Equally suitable either raw or cooked. Sieve cooked tomato to remove the seeds. Or scald and peel raw tomato, cut out the core, then mash. (You can remove the seeds if you like, but the jelly around them is a valuable source of soluble fiber.)
Grated apple or pear	Choose sweet apples and well-ripened pears. Peel and grate finely.
Peaches, apricots, nectarines, sweet cherries, plums, mangoes, papaya, kiwi fruit	Choose really ripe fruit. Remove the skin and pits; mash the flesh thoroughly.
Avocado	Cut in half. Scoop out and mash a little of the flesh, adding a few drops of boiled water to soften if necessary.
Broccoli, cauliflower, Brussels sprouts, green cabbage	Wash and trim. Cook in a minimum of unsalted water until tender (mashable but not soggy). Puree with a little of their cooking water. (Cooked cabbage and sprouts can create intestinal gas; if this is a problem, mix with another vegetable puree, such as carrot.)
Spinach	Wash thoroughly, remove the stems, shred the leaves. Cook in a saucepan without extra water until spinach is tender. Puree. (Don't give more than once or twice a week since the oxalic acid content affects the body's absorption of some minerals.)

FOOD	PREPARATION
Dried apricots, prunes, pears, peaches, apples	Wash, then cover with boiling water and soak overnight. Next day, simmer until tender. Remove pits from prunes. Puree the fruit. (Can have rather a laxative effect.)
Baby rice cereal	This is best as a first cereal because it is the least likely to cause allergic reactions. Choose one fortified with additional iron and B vitamins, and make up with liquid according to directions on the package.
Potatoes	Scrub. Bake or boil in unsalted water. Scoop potato out of skin and mash. A little very finely grated cheese, pot cheese, cottage cheese, yogurt, tofu, milk or soy milk can be added; also very finely chopped green vegetables, such as watercress or raw spinach leaves.
Corn, peas, green beans	Boil until tender; puree. Fresh or frozen are fine; canned are not advised because of the added salt and sugar.
Muesli	Buy a mix without sugar and other additives, or make your own from oats, nuts, and raisins, then grind to a powder. Moisten with water, fruit juice, or plain yogurt. Sprinkle with wheat germ and mix well. Powdered nuts or seeds or grated apple or pear can be added.
Whole wheat bread	From six months onwards, a little crustless bread can be added to vegetable purees. The bran in 100% whole wheat bread and flour is too laxative for some babies; an 81-85% bread (preferably with added wheat germ, for extra iron) is often a better choice for babies under two years old.

foods containing gluten. Foods least likely to cause an allergic reaction are rice, oats, root and leafy vegetables, apples and pears, dried fruit, beans and legumes. Signs of an allergic reaction are rashes and swelling of the eyes, lips and face; sickness; diarrhea; eczema; hay fever and asthma. Many so-called allergies are simply food intolerances which disappear as babies get older, usually by the time they are about two years old, although some, particularly to nuts and dairy products, can last for life. Whether or not you have a history of allergies, asthma, and eczema in your family, it's a good idea to try your baby on the same food for at least four days before trying another, so that you can be sure there are no adverse effects. Watch your baby carefully, and if all is well, try her on something else.

Preparing and Freezing Babyfood

Although it is impractical to sterilize all your kitchen equipment when you are preparing babyfood, it is important to be scrupulous about hygiene, especially in the early days. Dip your baby's spoon in a little boiling water to sterilize it before giving her juice or boiled water. Sterilize with feeding bottle sterilizer any plastic or glass bowls that you are using to prepare her food, and the little dish, cup or plate on which you put your baby's first tastes of

playing around by you while you're cooking. Have some way of blocking off the stairs. It takes a bit of an effort to do this, but is worthwhile because once it is done you can relax and let your baby race around and explore in safety while you get on with things.

Put your baby in old, comfy clothes so that she can get as grubby as she likes. The more unrestricted she is, the better for her development. For this reason it's not a good idea to leave a baby in a playpen for long periods of time (though a playpen can be useful for short periods, to provide a brief respite from being "on guard" all the time – long enough to answer the phone or drink a cup of tea, for instance). In general, however, it's not easy for a baby to learn to be an enquiring, hopeful, and enterprising adult if her efforts to explore are frustrated or, worst of all, rewarded with a slap. A baby of this age is too young to understand the meaning of punishment and will just be puzzled that the person to whom she looks for comfort and love has suddenly lashed out and hurt her.

Of course, however carefully you "baby-proof" your home, there will inevitably be times when she will get something she mustn't have, or manage to open a drawer which had hitherto been beyond her. When removing the forbidden treasures, it saves a great deal of hassle and upset if you can divert with an alternative: "You mustn't have that, but here's something that's just as much fun." If there are

certain things in the house which you do not want your toddler to touch, by all means explain this to her simply, but you will have to do so over and over again. It's unrealistic to expect a baby of this age to remember, or to override her own will/ need/desire; she is incapable of this until she is coming out of toddlerhood. Until then, her will and yours may coincide, but she is not capable of doing something to please you, or to annoy you. You really can't expect a baby or toddler to be aware of the consequences of her actions.

Hygiene

Once your baby is crawling around you may wonder about hygiene, especially as her presence means you're probably not able to clean the house as thoroughly as you'd like! Yet, as long as basic standards of hygiene are maintained, your baby will be fine. Keep the food-preparation areas of the house clean, also the bathroom, and keep pet food (which, like any food, can harbor bacteria) out of the way. Get the vet to worm your pets before your baby starts to crawl and then regularly every few months.

However clean you keep the house, once your baby is crawling around she will certainly need a bath in the evening to clean off the results of the day's explorations. Bathtime can be great fun with a variety of plastic ducks and containers, a lightweight plastic jug and funnel and a watering can for discovering the fascinations of water-play.

Entertaining Your Baby

During this period your baby will still enjoy the toys mentioned in the previous chapter (pp. 46-7). She will particularly appreciate toys which make a noise, such as drums, some bells or a tambourine. She will also have fun with toys which she can operate herself: a simple, not-too-noisy jack-in-the-box, a jumping man on a string, a wooden hen which clucks as you pull it along. Look for robust toys that are simple to operate. Once your baby can sit up, she will get a great deal of pleasure from playing in a sandbox. It's not difficult to make one by filling a large, shallow, wooden or plastic box with sand, or by digging one in the garden. Make sure you get "silver sand" from a garden or hardware store. Supply some small light spades or big spoons and a variety of containers for filling with sand, and always cover the sandbox with a lid or piece of plastic when it's not in use to keep cats out.

It's amazing how many toys a baby of this age accumulates, and you'll need to find somewhere indoors to keep these. A practical solution is a wicker or plastic laundry basket or a shallow wooden box into which you can heap everything after use, and from which it's easy for your baby to get what she wants during the day. Alternatively, you could use cheap, oblong, plastic washing-up bowls which can be stored on open shelving later on. Whichever you use, keep the box, basket or bowls of toys in the kitchen, sitting room or wherever you are during the day, so that your baby can play close to you.

Sharing Activities

"Close to you," not to say all over you, is the operative expression during this stage. You will find that you cope best if you can accept this, plan your activities with this in mind, and draw your baby into as many of them as possible. This can be frustrating, because everything will be accomplished much more slowly and less efficiently. The key is not to set your standards too high; mentally to slow down your own pace and remember that all the time you're in fact doing two jobs – the practical task in hand, and the most important job, that of looking after your baby. She will love to help dust the furniture and sweep the floor; to stand up at the sink on a chair and dabble her hands in the water while you're washing up; to play with some pastry trimmings when you're baking. A trip to the shops can be the highlight of her day, especially if you talk to her about all the interesting things you pass on the way, and the goods you're putting into your cart. Let your baby feel the bulkiness of a loaf of bread, the coldness of a packet of frozen peas, the lightness of a packet of potato chips. Then when you get home, let her help you to unpack your bags and put the things away. Make every effort to build up a feeling of the two of you as a team, coping with things together – and having fun together – rather than getting into the habit of thinking of your baby as an impediment preventing you from doing what you want to do. A warm feeling of companionship created now will grow and stand you in good stead for the future.

What with the clutter which a baby makes about the house and the demands she makes on your time, unless you have a great deal of domestic help it's impossible to maintain high standards of tidiness and housekeeping. This is easier if you're not terribly houseproud than if you're naturally inclined to worry about every mark. But you will be far happier – and so will your baby – if you can resign yourself to having just a quick tidy-up once a day than if you feel that things ought to be tidier all the time. Why? Who for? The most important thing at this stage is for your baby to be happy and for you to relax and enjoy her.

When my babies reached this stage I found that, in contrast to the early baby days, I coped best if I had some sort of routine to the day. Periods of play with bricks, sand, water, quiet times looking at picture books and playing with other toys, interspersed with walks to the shops or the park or to feed the ducks, and a blessed period in the late morning or early afternoon when the baby slept.

If you are at home all day you are quite likely to find that coping with a lively "into everything" baby, doing the essential shopping, making an evening meal and keeping the house in some sort of rough order occupies your whole day and takes every ounce of energy, leaving you exhausted in the evening with very little to show for your labors except one happy, thriving, rosy-cheeked little person.

Going Back to Work

Much the same could be said about tiredness if you are working full-time or part-time. Here your major concern will be balancing the demands of your job with the many needs of your family and at times you will feel stretched to the limit. On top of this, you will probably feel guilty for leaving your baby. But returning to work has both positive and negative aspects, so try and accept this without regrets. As my birth counselor, Gill Thorn, says:

> The popular image of an organized woman with her family life under control so that it never interferes with her work is a myth. The best you can hope for is that your arrangements hold up most of the time. You'll juggle work and motherhood and may feel that you are doing neither job well; your baby will probably be perfectly happy!

Getting your support network and childcare arrangements sorted out so that you are completely happy with them is of course a priority. Helpful books and information on this are available (see Useful Addresses). You need to think about it at an early stage – while you are still pregnant is not too early – particularly if you want your baby to go to a good day-care center. If you know in advance what sort of hours you want to work, and you think your employer would be open to such ideas, it might be worth discussing your plans in advance. Make sure that you familiarize yourself with company policy on maternity leave and maternity pay beforehand.

Clingy Babies

It is hard that the time for returning to work often coincides with a natural phase in your baby's development when they become fiercely attached to you. They can become very upset every time they lose sight of you, even if it is only for a few moments. This phase passes quickly if you give your baby the reassurance she needs by staying with her as much as possible. She cannot understand that if you go away you will come back: she does not know enough. The more you try to stop her from clinging by going away, the more insecure and fearful she will get. Even if you are planning to be at home full-time, it's a good idea to get her used to another person: perhaps a relative or neighbor whom she knows well enough to be left with when you have to go away for short periods. On the other hand, it is obviously best if you can keep the times when you're away from your baby to the minimum while this "clingy" period lasts. By giving her what she needs during this intensely emotional time you'll help it to pass as speedily as possible. You will also create an emotional security which will enable your baby to make happy and fulfilling relationships throughout her future life.

If you are planning to return to work, it is important to give your baby plenty of time to adjust to her sitter, nursemaid or carer at the nursery. Leave your baby for an hour or so to begin with, gradually building up to a full day over a period of weeks if you can. That way your baby will come to know her "substitute mom" and know that you always come back. You, in turn, will feel relaxed and happy, knowing that your baby is settled. Don't expect to feel quite "normal" when you return to work; remember you have been through a major experience and that you are still adjusting mentally, emotionally and physically. Just treat yourself gently and keep reminding yourself, "I'm doing the best I can."

Feeding Problems

Some babies are very fussy eaters which makes mothers worry, wondering how they can tell if their baby is getting enough food. If your baby is healthy, lively, and growing, then you can be sure that enough food is being consumed even if it seems like too little.

Do not worry if your baby really does not like some food, because you can usually find another source of the same nutrients (see pp. 84-5). It is far better to stick to foods which you know your baby likes – and avoid battles of will. And do not worry if your baby eats her food in the "wrong" order or mixes things up. As long as she's eating nutritious foods, it really doesn't matter how she eats them.

It also helps if you can encourage your baby to feed herself from an early age. Protect her clothes with a sensible bib – the plastic ones with pockets in which to catch spilled food are good – and the floor under the high chair with newspaper, which looks messy but can be thrown away and renewed, or with plastic sheeting, which has to be wiped clean. Put the food in front of your baby and let her feed herself. This will be an undeniably messy business at first but it will be worth it in the end and with practice her competence will grow.

Sleeping

Babies need less sleep in their second six months, and if yours is a particularly lively baby you may soon find her sleeping time during the day reduced to two short periods or one longer one (if that!). Whether your baby actually sleeps or not, it's a good idea to plan your day to include two brief "rest" times, when you settle her into her baby carriage or crib. Provide plenty of interesting things for her to look at or get on with quietly until she actually falls asleep. But if she doesn't go to sleep, make sure that you do not leave her to "rest" for too long, so that she starts to become bored and unhappy.

During this period, often around nine months, many babies go through a phase of being difficult at bedtime. A baby who has hitherto gone to bed quite happily will become very clingy, screaming, crying and not wanting you to leave the room. This is really a night-time extension of the emotional clinging described on p. 59. Once again, the quickest way to get through this stage is to give your baby the comfort she needs and assure her of your physical closeness. But at the same time you have to ease yourself away, or you will find yourself trapped into sitting with your baby until she falls asleep – which could be quite a lengthy process.

Preparing for Bedtime

Prepare for bedtime by making the hour preceding it as happy and loving as possible. Try to avoid upsets and conflicts at this time. Warn your baby that bedtime is approaching and build up a bedtime routine that you follow each day: perhaps a pleasant bath, playing with the ducks and other toys in the water, then a trip downstairs to say "goodnight" to the rest of the family. Then up to the bedroom for a story, a "goodnight" kiss for the favorite toys, a kiss and a cuddle for your baby and a favorite lullaby. After this, tell your baby that she must go to sleep, that you're going downstairs but you'll pop back in a moment or two. Keep popping back and also calling out encouragingly as necessary. If your baby really won't release you, it may be helpful if you can arrange to delay your parting by planning to tidy and put away clothes in her bedroom so that you're close while she is going off to sleep. Go out when this is done, but again, keeping popping back reassuringly often, and certainly either pop back or call out reassuringly if your baby cries out. This way you'll build up her confidence that you're still there and that her needs will be answered, and gradually the difficult phase will pass. Whatever you do, try not to pick your baby up and bring her downstairs, even once, as this will create bad habits for the future. You've got to be loving but firm; which isn't always easy – I think we're often afraid to be firm, but it can be done in a kind and loving way, reassuring your baby at the same time that you're still close and caring, but also that you're not going to pick her up or play!

Waking at Night

Sometimes a restless, wakeful pattern may develop during the night around this time, too. This can be extremely wearying when you're physically exhausted by the demands of a lively and increasingly mobile baby. Often there is no apparent reason for the wakefulness, but it's worth checking the obvious things such as whether your baby is warm enough – one of those "baby bags" will keep her cosy if she kicks the covers off; whether there is some noise that is waking her up and, if so, whether you can improve the situation by moving her bed to a different position, putting up thicker curtains or even double-glazing; whether she is waking because of diaper rash making her bottom sore (protect her with a thick layer of cream and a one-way diaper at bedtime). You might also like to try giving your baby a few drops of a harmless, natural, sleeping remedy at bedtime. There's one called Avena Sativa Compound which is manufactured by Weleda and obtainable from health stores.

If none of these things makes any difference, it's quite tempting to think that your baby is waking herself up on purpose, just to be annoying. This of course is impossible: just think how difficult it is for adults to wake themselves up by strength of will, let alone a tiny baby! Neither can babies of this age do things for effect, either to annoy or please you. They can, however, do things because your response amuses or interests them, so don't reward a wakeful baby by being chatty or scolding.

There may be some subtle reason for your baby's restlessness. It may be that she unconsciously feels the need for more cuddling, or is upset by something in her day's routine. Sometimes this night-time waking is associated with trying to wean a baby too quickly, for instance, when she still needs the comfort of sucking. So mentally check on these things next. If none of these applies – or the problem is no better – there is nothing you can do but accept the situation and make the best of it. It may be helpful to find out whether it works best to leave the baby to cry for ten minutes –

some give up and go back to sleep – or go in immediately. If you have the kind of baby that you have to go in to, you'll probably find it best to get up quickly, the moment she starts to cry. She will probably go back to sleep quickly as soon as she's reassured of your presence, and you too can go back to bed and, with any luck, also fall asleep again quickly.

My third child woke up usually five times a night until she was 18 months old – when she suddenly started sleeping through – so I have great sympathy for this problem. I coped by going to my child as soon as she cried, sending her back to sleep with a breastfeed – which was usually extremely quick – and then thankfully going straight back to sleep myself. It's amazing how quickly one learns to go to sleep after these night-time interruptions. They are tiresome: but, like most of the difficult stages, they do pass!

Waking Too Early

Some babies wake at a most unsociably early time in the morning and this too can be a problem. But it's no good expecting a baby refreshed by a night's sleep to go back to sleep again. It's better to arrange for the room to be lit with a low-power night-light and leave some suitable toys within reach. It may even be worth making the effort to get up and give her a drink or change her diaper, if this will mean she will play happily in her crib for a while and give you a little longer in bed.

When Your Baby is Six to Eight Months Old

You will find that as your baby takes more solid food, her demand for milk will decrease. Your baby will suck from you for a shorter time and, at around eight or nine months, may eventually give up the milk feed entirely. Your milk supply will decline correspondingly; the reverse of the process that enabled you to produce enough milk in the early days. You will probably find it takes two or three days for your body to catch up with your baby's decreased demand, and your breasts may feel rather full, but this transition period only lasts for a few days.

You can now begin to enrich the simple fruit and vegetable purees with vegetarian protein ingredients. Any of the foods shown opposite can be added.

Once your baby is taking these solids happily, you can give an enriched vegetable puree as a main course, followed by a fruit puree or yogurt- or cereal-based mixture as a "dessert." You can also begin introducing solids before the other main feeds of the day, so that eventually the feeds that correspond to breakfast, lunch, and supper are composed entirely of solids. You will also find that, as your baby gets used to the texture of solid foods, there is no need to be so particular about pureeing the food. In fact it is good for her to get used to a bit of texture in food at this stage. I soon found I only needed to mash food for my babies, although I know other babies can

VEGETARIAN PROTEIN ENRICHMENT FOODS FOR WEANING

FOOD	PREPARATION
Orange lentils	Made into a thick soup, as described on p. 101, these make a wonderfully nutritious meal for a baby. Serve as it is, or with a little crustless whole wheat bread mashed into it; or make soup extra thick and add to a vegetable puree.
Mashed beans	Use home-cooked beans (soy beans, red kidney, cannellini, baked beans, etc), or canned ones, well-rinsed, to remove salted water. (Don't use canned ones before baby is eight months old.) Mash thoroughly or puree.
Beans in tomato sauce	These make a quick and nutritious meal from eight months onward. Choose a variety without preservatives or colorings. (They will probably include a little salt and sugar; despite this, they're still a healthy and nutritious food.) Mash or puree. Can be mixed with crumbled whole-wheat bread and a little boiled water to moisten.
Tofu	Drain tofu, mash thoroughly, then mix with vegetable or fruit purees.
Tahini, smooth peanut butter	Mix a little – perhaps $1/2$ teaspoon at first – into vegetable or fruit purees. Choose a smooth peanut butter without salt or additives, such as emulsifiers and stabilizers.
Yeast extract	Use a low-sodium one from the health food store. Add a little – $1/4$ teaspoon at first – to vegetable purees.
Nutritional yeast flakes	Use a debittered brand, and sprinkle sparingly – just a pinch – over baby's vegetable purees or breakfast muesli mix. Can also be added to a mashed-banana-and-yogurt mix.
Finely milled nuts and seeds	Powder the nuts in a blender, food processor or clean electric coffee grinder, or use ground almonds. If you're grinding your own, use a variety of nuts – almonds, Brazil nuts, peanuts, walnuts, pumpkin, and sunflower seeds – for a full range of nutrients. Stir into fruit or vegetable purees, starting with $1/2$ teaspoonful.
Wheat germ	Sprinkle sparingly over fruit or vegetable purees; add to cereal mixes and yogurt for splendid nourishment.
Cottage cheese; low-fat soft white cheeses such as ricotta	Give this from eight months, choosing one that's preservative-free, low-salt, and, in the case of cottage cheese, not too lumpy. Mash into fruit or vegetable purees; or mix with finely shredded watercress or very finely grated carrot and cheese, a little wheat germ, some nutritional yeast flakes, or yeast extract for a healthy baby salad mix!
Hard cheese	Choose a low-fat hard cheese if possible, with no colorings or preservatives. Grate finely; add to pureed vegetables, starting with $1/2$ teaspoonful.

/Continued on p.64

FOOD	PREPARATION
Yogurt	Choose an active plain yogurt without preservatives. Add to fruit purees or give as it is, with a little Date Spread (p. 88) stirred in and a sprinkling of wheat germ and/or powdered nuts. Mashed with banana and wheat germ, and perhaps a little tahini, and some powdered nuts, this makes a quick baby meal.
Eggs	Eggs always need to be thoroughly cooked to avoid the risk of salmonella. You could try mashing the yolk of a hard-cooked egg into a vegetable puree. If this goes down well, try well-cooked scrambled eggs. Don't introduce egg until your baby is 18 to 24 months old if there is any history of allergies, eczema or asthma in the family.

be more fussy. You will gradually be able to drop first one milk feed and then another, so that by the time your baby is around nine months the bedtime feed may well be the only one left. Do not be in a hurry to wean your baby from the bliss of this, especially if you are working during the day; it is important for the closeness to you and the emotional satisfaction the sucking gives. Many babies have spontaneously given up the bedtime feed by the time they are one year old, but many have not.

Some people believe it is not a good thing to encourage feeding during the night after, say, six months, when your baby probably doesn't need it for nourishment but may just be acquiring an enjoyable habit that may drive you to distraction later on.

Other childcare experts would disagree with this approach and I personally feel that if a child cries for food (and the loving comfort of her mother's closeness), then it is better to meet that need, even though this can be a demanding period.

But it does pass and, I believe, contributes very much to the child's emotional security both at the time and, more especially, in later life.

At this stage, particularly if your baby is teething, you can introduce some finger foods. Your baby may find it comforting to chew on something hard: a piece of apple, raw carrot, bread or rusk, but never leave a baby alone with food like this because of the danger of choking; if anything gets stuck in your baby's throat, be ready either to hook it out quickly with your finger or else turn her upside down and smack her *gently* in the small of the back until the object is dislodged.

Suggested Feeding Pattern, from Six to Eight Months Old

● On waking: Breast/bottlefeed

● Breakfast: Baby rice or muesli cereal or enriched fruit puree; breast/bottlefeed

● Mid-morning: Diluted fruit juice from

a spoon or cup (or give this drink mid-afternoon)

- Lunch: 1-2 tablespoons enriched vegetable puree, or lentil puree, followed by some fruit puree for dessert (optional); breast/ bottlefeed – until your baby gives this up

- Mid-afternoon: Diluted fruit juice from spoon or cup (unless this was given in the morning) Finger foods: slices of apple, carrot sticks, whole wheat rusk

- Dinner: Same as breakfast; breast/bottlefeed

- Before bed: Breast/bottlefeed

When Your Baby is Eight to Twelve Months Old

If your baby takes well to solids, you will quite soon find that she will easily and naturally eat a little of what you, as a family, are having. If you're in doubt about the suitability of certain foods, check them against the "Cautionary Notes" on p. 78. The main thing to watch is that your baby's portion is not too highly seasoned or salted. Sometimes it's possible to take out a small quantity for your baby before adding spices and seasonings.

If your baby gets used to trying new flavors, it will make it possible for you to eat out with friends or in a restaurant. Simply select a suitably unspiced or lightly seasoned dish from the menu – again, check the suitability of various foods – or ask for an unsalted omelet or just vegetables and grated cheese, and mash your baby's portion with a fork.

At this stage you may need to consider the amount of fiber your baby is getting. Since a vegetarian diet is naturally high in fiber, which facilitates the passage of food through the intestines, it's important for your baby to have some concentrated sources of nourishment each day as well, such as egg, cheese, yogurt, powdered nuts, yeast and yeast extract (unsalted), tahini, and peanut butter. If your baby's diet becomes too laxative, it can cause a very sore bottom. In this case it may be advisable to give a bread that is lower in fiber than whole wheat. Try wheat germ bread, or, if this is still too fibrous, get an enriched white one. Try a higher-fiber bread again when your baby is a little older.

At this stage, between nine months and one year, your baby will probably have an eating plan that goes something like this:

Suggested Feeding Pattern, from Eight or Nine Months On

- On waking: Water or diluted fruit juice from cup

- Breakfast: Muesli, Crunchy Version (p. 17) or oatmeal; whole wheat toast or bread with low-sodium yeast extract

- Mid-morning: Diluted fruit juice

- Lunch: Mashed nut or legume savory with vegetables; fruit puree and cereal pudding or fruit with yogurt or custard; water or milk

- Mid-afternoon: Diluted fruit juice; finger foods (e.g. slices of apple, carrot sticks, whole wheat rusk)

- Dinner: Whole wheat bread with cottage cheese, nut butter or lentil spread; or scrambled egg on bread or toast; or Very Quick Lentil Soup (p. 101) with whole wheat bread; carrot sticks, pieces of raw cucumber, slices of apple; fruit with yogurt or cereal pudding as at lunch; water or milk

- Before bed: Breast/bottlefeed

The Vegetarian Toddler

This second year marks the transition from babyhood to the toddler stage and great progress is made. It's a delightful and interesting period during which your baby learns a large number of new skills and becomes even more of a companion.

In many ways a one- to two-year-old is still very much a baby; yet at the same time she feels a growing awareness of her own identity and need for independence. It can therefore also be quite a turbulent time for you both, and humor and a philosophical attitude, plus plenty of patience, will help you to cope. The secret during this period – and indeed throughout childhood – lies in being sensitive to your child's needs; being careful not to push her towards independence too quickly, yet at the same time avoiding treating her too much as a baby and so causing rebellion and aggression.

You are still the center of your toddler's life and she is just beginning to learn that she wants to please you. Before, she was not aware of you as a person separate from her. Yet, on the other hand, she feels an increasing need for independence and may suffer an inner conflict as a result. You can help by gently teaching her to be independent, being sensitive both to her need and her capability, helping her to cope with each stage as soon as she is ready, but without pushing her faster than she can manage to go. Praise her for being, full stop. That is, praise her for what she is, not what she does. That way she cannot fail, and she will learn what pleases you by your attitude, not your words. Watch that you do not inadvertently put pressure on her so that she feels she has to reach an impossible standard in order to get your approval.

Children – even within the same family – are so different and I think one of the secrets of successful handling is to be able to let your child set the pace while being on the lookout for signs that she is ready to be helped to cope with a new skill.

I know this is a controversial subject, but I must say I found it very helpful with my own children to know a little about their type of character and temperament from their horoscope. I found the information which this gave extremely valuable; in fact I wouldn't like to have to bring up a child without it! The information is general enough to avoid molding the child in a preconceived way but gives many helpful pointers for bringing the best out of the particular temperament which, by the age of two, it's becoming obvious that the child has. The address to write to for more information is on the fourth page of this book.

Play and Development

During this year physical skills increase dramatically and you'll need to expand the boundaries of your baby's safe play-area accordingly. Try, as before, to make the area safe and baby-proof rather than have the worry of the possibility of the toddler getting into danger or mischief, or the strain of constantly having to restrict her or say "no." Be clear in your own mind about where you will draw the boundaries, but have as few of these as possible. Remember, toddlers have short memories, strong emotions and live in the present; a child of this age simply does not understand the difference between "being good" and "being naughty," so do not expect the impossible.

Encouraging Independence

Make sure your toddler is not thwarted in her movements by clothes which are stiff, uncomfortable, or too big. They should be soft and comfortable to wear so that they don't restrict vigorous play; have easy-care things which can go straight into the machine and don't need ironing. At this stage of rapid growth it's a waste of money to buy special clothes for best. Buy normal clothes which you can use for best when they're new, then for everyday wear after that. Cheap and cheerful, easy-to-do-up, washable, drip-dry clothes are the best choice from both your point of view and your toddler's, with a washable all-in-one snow suit for cold days and rubber boots for splashing through puddles. Apart from the fun of playing with sand, water, and mud, a toddler can only concentrate on one thing at a time and if she is busy trying to climb up a muddy bank she won't be able to think about keeping her clothes clean.

Make the most of your child's urge for independence and help her to achieve it.

Show her, for instance, how to slide safely off the bed by rolling on to her tummy and sliding off, feet first, and how to negotiate the stairs safely. When you're showing your toddler how to do something, make a conscious effort to slow your pace right down. We take familiar actions, such as doing up a button or tying shoelaces, so much for granted, forgetting how many small actions are involved in the process. Try doing things with the other hand from the one you naturally use to get an idea of how your toddler, with her lack of coordination, feels. Break up each process into tiny stages and teach these to your child slowly, one at a time, so she gradually learns the complete skill.

Encouraging Curiosity

Every day is full of discovery for a child of this age and it is a revelation to see the apparently boring daily walk to the shops through her eyes. You suddenly find yourself noticing all kinds of things such as fire trucks and car-transporters, and it becomes so automatic to point these out that you may find yourself doing so to an amazed company of adults when your toddler isn't with you! Even visits to the supermarket can be fun if you let your baby take a lively interest in your shopping. Talk about the things you're buying, enlist her "help" over what you need, which item to choose, then let her examine the things as you put them in the shopping cart.

As a change from the daily routine, toddlers love trips to different places: a visit to a farm or zoo, a trip on a train or bus for a change from the car. These will stimulate her interest and give plenty for her to look at and point. You can help the development of her language by talking about the things that you see, drawing her attention to different colors and shapes.

Encouraging Individuality

Help your toddler begin to make decisions by asking her to make simple choices (and stick to them!): "Which sock shall we put on first?" or "Which color brick shall we pick up next?" It's best to avoid presenting her with complicated choices where she hasn't the experience to know which she'd enjoy most and will worry that she's going to make, or has made, the wrong choice. To ask "Would you like to go to the park and play on the swings or go to the pond and feed the ducks?" is probably too difficult for her; it's better to say "Let's go to the park and play on the swings" and save the alternative for another day.

It's good experience, too, for your toddler to have the chance to play with another child of her own age. "Playing together" at this stage usually only amounts to toddlers watching one another, and for the most part each getting on with their own activities, with you intervening fairly frequently when one takes the other's toy. Babies become very possessive about their toys at this stage, and your efforts to take something away will be met with howls of rage. So always be quick to offer an alternative toy or activity.

Toys for Toddlers

Regarding suitable toys for this age group, your toddler will still have fun with all the toys mentioned in the previous sections. Water play, the sandbox and play with bricks will be specially enjoyed; also cups or rings which stack into or on to each other and teach the first concept of bigger and smaller. With these your toddler will also be able to learn the meaning of into and on to, inside and outside, through putting things into boxes and playing hide-and-seek with her toys. Toys which push and pull along are great fun; also a posting box, which teaches the recognition of different shapes; simple jigsaws and tray jigsaws. A large cardboard box which she can crawl into will give her hours of fun.

Discipline and Punishment

What is discipline? Not punishment, but teaching. I, personally, am not in favor of spanking children, especially when they're as young as this. When a baby or young child looks to you for love and comfort, it seems to me to be abusing that trust suddenly to inflict physical pain on the child. And it's equally bad to discipline a young child by putting emotional pressure on her; pretending to cry if she does something naughty; giving warmth and love when she is "good" and being cool when

she is "naughty." A baby of this age is too young to understand the consequences of her actions, that if she pulls the tablecloth everything will fall on to the floor, if she drops your best vase it will break.

Even if she did understand these things, her memory is short and a toddler lives very much in the present. So although she may promise not to pull out your drawer of sewing things again – and mean it at the time – a few minutes afterwards she will have forgotten all about it and will undoubtedly do it again later. To scold her for it would be confusing because she has genuinely forgotten about the last time – and is too little to understand the concept of "promise," anyway. It's better to secure the drawer or move your sewing things to a higher one and put some bricks or other toys in the one she keeps opening.

This second course of action is the best because not only does it harmonize the situation, it also gives your baby the satisfaction of being able to do something for herself – to open "her" drawer and get some toys out. This demonstrates one of the secrets of handling a toddler: avoid confrontation whenever possible and look for a positive way of dealing with a situation. If she gets something she can't have, divert her with something else that's "much more fun;" if you want her to fetch something and she says "no," challenge her to a race: "I bet you can't get it before I've counted to five." She'll get it, "win," and have fun at the same time. Once you get into the habit of thinking in these ways it's surprising how many potentially difficult situations can be turned into fun. This way you can make your toddler do what you want her to do.

Coping with Tantrums

If you adopt the policies described above, you will (mostly) avoid exhausting tantrums and the bond between you will grow stronger and warmer as you "have fun" together and generally meet life's challenges as a team. However, there will almost certainly be times when you or your baby are tired and you mismanage or misjudge the situation, or when things are complicated by some other factor and a tantrum results. Once the child is in the grip of a tantrum, she is coping with an emotional force too strong to control. She is incapable of stopping and may be frightened by the strength of her own emotions. She may shout and scream and rush around the room, crashing into everything that's in her path, or throw herself to the floor, kicking and screaming. She may even stop breathing and appear to lose consciousness briefly, though pediatricians assure us that children cannot permanently damage themselves this way.

During the Tantrum

Keep as calm as you can when dealing with this situation; try at all costs to avoid screaming back at your child even though you, too, feel at the end of your tether.

When she is in the grip of a tantrum she genuinely cannot do anything about it. Take immediate steps to remove anything dangerous or breakable. It's generally best to hold your child firmly either on the floor, if that is where she has ended up, or on your lap. Then she will gradually calm down and can be cuddled and comforted. If holding your child only makes the tantrum worse, just move anything dangerous or breakable out of the way and wait until she has calmed down before cuddling and comforting her.

After the Tantrum

Go ahead with whatever you had planned; don't alter your plans in response to the tantrum or punish the child by stopping an activity she enjoys. Let her see that you accept the tantrum as something which she cannot help. Try not to reward her with extra (disapproving) attention after a tantrum; do not let her see that you're upset by them or worried about the possibility of her having one in an awkward place. Try not, for instance, to treat her any differently if she has a tantrum when you're visiting a very prim and proper friend than you would do if it happened at home. I realize that's difficult, because most of us are so aware of the disapproval of others and this does change our behavior; but that's the ideal to aim for! Continue to do your best to handle your toddler in such a way as to avoid tantrums as much as possible, but to treat them as calmly and matter-of-factly as you can when they do arise, and very soon you'll find you're through this stage.

Resting and Sleeping

This is often an inbetween period for rests as your toddler makes the transition from two naps a day to one long one and you will probably find yourself constantly adjusting your timetable and the hour at which you have your lunch. Many toddlers end up having quite a long rest in the middle of the day, then as they get older they want to go down for this later and later so that it begins to interfere with bedtime. When this happens your toddler may have to be woken from her rest before she's really ready. Most toddlers hate being woken up from a rest and you'll need to allow time for cuddles and comforts as you gently help your toddler to ease herself into the waking world again.

Bedtime can still be a problem for a baby of this age, with difficulty in getting her to settle down and go to sleep and begging you to stay. I do not hold with the "leave her to cry whatever happens" philosophy; I think it's best to aim for an extension of the policy described in the previous chapter. Follow a soothing bedtime ritual, as described on p.60, spend a little time tidying or pottering about, in or close to your toddler's bedroom, then say a final "goodnight" and go. But be prepared to go straight back if your toddler starts to cry seriously (as against one or two sleepy cries).

When you go back, reassure your child that you're still there, that she hasn't been deserted. Having done this in a cheerful but firm manner, go out again. If you keep this up long enough she will get bored, yet at the same time she will finally drop off to sleep with the comforting thought that you're not far away and that you care. Some toddlers take an awful long time to get bored! So aim to do the very minimum necessary to reassure your child: you have to use trial and error to discover what this is. Trying though it is, this phase also passes and you'll soon have forgotten all about it.

Nightmares

Sometimes during this year a toddler goes through a phase of waking up, terrified, with nightmares. When this happens, all you can do is to go to her, cuddle and reassure her until she's comforted, then settle her back to sleep. But it's worth thinking about any possible reason for these disturbances. Is she going through a particularly stressful period, for some reason? And if so, can you think of any ways of taking the pressure off? Perhaps she is being weaned too quickly or is anxious because of overzealous potty training? Perhaps her routine has been disrupted in some way, or maybe there is a new baby in the family? Be extra loving and tolerant, take special care to keep to her familiar routine and generally "baby" her a bit, until her sense of security returns.

Potty Training

Since a child is physiologically unable to control her bladder and bowels until 15 months at the very earliest, there's absolutely no point in starting potty training, or even buying a potty before then. The important thing with potty training is to relax – and let it happen. Remember that babies vary a good deal in the time it takes them to get "clean" and "dry," and if your particular child is later than some it's no reflection on either you or her. It's not a race, and all babies get potty-trained eventually, even though you may begin to wonder whether yours is going to be the great exception!

To start with, babies are totally unaware of their bodily functions. Then, suddenly one day, when your toddler is about to have a dirty diaper, she notices the physical sensation and realizes that something is about to happen, though not soon enough to stop. Once this has happened, you can produce the potty and suggest next time she might try going in that instead of in her diaper. But don't appear too eager: try and be fairly unemotional about the whole thing. You will find your toddler will get the idea.

Toddlers are able to control their bowels first; bladder control takes longer, because the sensation of passing water,

especially into a damp diaper, isn't so noticeable. It will help your toddler to become aware of what is happening if you can let her have some periods of play without a diaper. It's a great help if this stage coincides with some warm summer weather and your toddler can run about in the garden without a diaper. Then, when she makes a puddle, she will suddenly notice what is happening. However, don't expect too much too soon, because noticing what is happening and actually being able to control it and reach the potty in time are two different things. You'll need plenty of patience, clean pants, and damp cloths to wipe up the many puddles. But gradually your toddler will get the idea of telling you – probably by clutching herself strategically – when she's about to make a puddle, and hang on long enough for you to reach the potty or toilet. You can, by the way, get a special children's toilet seat which fits over the ordinary one. Unless your toddler is frightened of the toilet, I don't think these are worth bothering with. It's better, in my opinion, to help her to get used to coping with the ordinary toilet as soon as possible.

Getting out of Diapers

Once you've got to this stage, I think it's best to abandon diapers in favor of terry-cloth pants or disposable training pants during the day, using a diaper just at night and if you're going out and don't want the risk of a puddle.

Much as you're longing to be rid of

diapers, do try not to get emotional about potty training. If you show pleasure when your toddler manages to use the potty, she has the means of displeasing you, and by this stage also the capability of using it. If you're having problems, not showing you're either pleased or displeased can defuse the situation. Accept it calmly when your toddler uses the potty, but equally accept that there are bound to be many "accidents" too. Try to be even-tempered about these, and certainly don't scold your toddler for them; she isn't doing it on purpose to be annoying, and she will get dry. Once she does, you'll find when you go out that you've simply swapped diaper-changing gear for a potty which you'll be taking everywhere with you, until she's got enough control to hang on while you find a toilet. People who haven't had this experience can have no idea how this searching-for-toilets stage slows up shopping expeditions and other trips: but, again, it doesn't last long.

Feeding Your Vegetarian Toddler

When a toddler is a fussy eater, I think it's best to let her eat when she wants to, rather than insist that everything has to be eaten at proper mealtimes. Don't worry that this will lead to bad habits; children are remarkably adaptable and she'll adjust to normal mealtimes later. I also think it's best to concentrate on giving a fussy toddler the food she likes, rather than insist on her eating things she's not keen on, with battles, and probably failure, as a result. Fussy children often do much better with raw finger food which they can eat with their fingers, rather than "proper" meals. They also frequently want to eat what appear to be funny mixtures of foods, or to have these in an unconventional order. But what does it matter if she wants cold red kidney beans with raisins or cold potato with peanut butter? As long as they're nutritious foods, why not? If you adopt this approach, while continuing to eat your own meals as normal, giving her some when it's something she'll eat and alternatives when it isn't, this phase will quickly pass.

Suggestions for Baby's and Toddler's Lunches

When you're preparing a midday meal for a baby or toddler, it's very convenient to be able to make something you can eat too. And it's got to be quick and easy! There are plenty of simple, delicious dishes that you can enjoy for lunch and share with your baby, either as they are or by adapting them slightly (suggestions for labor-saving shared meals opposite).

While babies will usually eat what they're given, often with great relish, when they get to the toddler stage (between 15 months and four years old) and develop minds of their own, feeding can become more of a problem. They often have passionate likes and dislikes, and I've met many mothers who are worried that their

LUNCHES YOU CAN SHARE WITH YOUR BABY OR TODDLER
(Dishes marked * are suitable for freezing)

YOUR LUNCH	BABY'S LUNCH	NOTES
Hot Potato Salad with Peanut Dressing (p. 100)	Mashed Hot Potato Salad with Peanut Dressing Carrot sticks and slices of apple	Be sure to use a smooth peanut butter without sugar, salt, or palm oil added.
Baked potato with grated cheese or mashed cooked beans Lettuce, tomato, and grated carrot Banana with yogurt and wheat germ	The inside of a baked potato, mashed with a little milk, grated cheese, or pureed cooked beans Banana mashed with a little yogurt and wheat germ Milk	Your baby can have a little very finely grated carrot and mashed skinned tomato mixed with the potato too.
Baked beans on whole wheat toast Watercress Sliced peach with yogurt, wheat germ, and chopped nuts	Baked beans mashed with crumbled whole wheat bread (soak in a little water if necessary to make bread mashable) Skinned peach mashed into yogurt, sprinkled with wheat germ Milk	Choose a brand of baked beans that does not have preservatives or colorings and preferably one that has reduced sugar and salt.
Very Quick Lentil Soup* (p. 101) with whole wheat roll Tomato and watercress Fresh fruit	Very Quick Lentil Soup with whole wheat bread mashed into it Fresh fruit pieces prepared for finger-feeding Milk	Freeze leftover soup in usable portions for future use.
Cheese or Tahini Dip (p. 90) sandwiches Tomatoes, lettuce, and carrot sticks Fresh fruit	Whole wheat bread mashed in a little warm milk or soy milk with grated cheese or Tahini Dip Fresh fruit, mashed, grated, or prepared for finger-feeding Milk	
Avocado filled with cottage cheese or Tahini Dip (p. 90) and shredded scallions, with lettuce, tomato, and watercress Fresh fruit	Avocado mashed with cottage cheese or Tahini Dip and very finely shredded watercress Fresh fruit, mashed, grated, or prepared for finger-feeding Milk	Choose a small, ripe avocado.
Hummus* (p. 91) with pita bread and sprigs of raw cauliflower and carrot sticks	Hummus with whole wheat bread mashed into it Sprigs of cauliflower and carrot sticks for finger-feeding Yogurt pureed with raisins Milk	Make or buy a hummus without much garlic. Soak the raisins in hot water or apple juice for 45 minutes or so beforehand.

/Continued on p. 76

YOUR LUNCH	BABY'S LUNCH	NOTES
Leftover Lentil and Broccoli Gratin* (p. 118) Lettuce and tomato Soaked dried apricots with yogurt	Leftover Lentil and Broccoli Gratin reheated and mashed with skinned tomato Soaked dried apricots pureed with yogurt, topped with wheat germ	Buy unsulfured dried apricots and soak overnight.
Red Kidney Bean and Avocado Salad (p. 99) on lettuce with tomato and grated carrot Whole wheat bread Apple, raw, or baked with filling of dates and wheat germ, topped with yogurt	Red kidney beans mashed with finely chopped lettuce and finely grated carrot Fingers of whole wheat bread or toast and yeast extract Finger-food slices of raw apple, or finely grated apple, or mashed baked apple and date with yogurt Milk	Canned beans (without coloring) are fine from eight months on. Put beans into a sieve and rinse under cold water to remove some of the brine.
Scrambled egg or Scrambled Tofu (p. 125) on whole wheat toast Watercress Orange	Scrambled egg or tofu on crumbled whole wheat toast Skinned orange sections for finger-feeding Milk	Remember to cook the egg thoroughly, to avoid the risk of salmonella!

toddler hardly seems to be eating enough to keep a sparrow alive. I've been through this stage with my own children, so I know the kind of inner panic that can easily set in as yet another meal is barely touched. Pediatricians say reassuringly that no child of this age will starve in the face of food, so if your child is obviously thriving, in spite of minuscule meals, then you do not have to worry too much. The most important thing is for you to remain calm and not allow a tense atmosphere to build up at mealtimes.

It is important with children of this age, even if their tastes are faddish, to make sure that everything they do eat is as nourishing as possible. One problem with a vegetarian/vegan diet is that many of the foods, although nutritious, are also rather high in fiber, and while that is a good thing for adults, young children may not be able to chew enough to obtain all the nutrients in a concentrated form.

Milk

If you can possibly do so, try to get your child to drink $2^1/2$ cups of whole (not skim or lowfat) milk or soy milk (use baby formula soy milk until your child is five years old) each day. This will ensure that her requirements for riboflavin and calcium are pretty well covered, as well as providing half or more of the day's protein, valuable zinc, vitamin A, and, in the case of soy milk, almost a quarter of the day's iron requirement. Milk or soy milk can of course be consumed in many other ways than as a plain drink; they can also be eaten in the form of yogurt, flavored and lightly sweetened if necessary; on breakfast cereals; as frothy milk shakes, ice-cream, puddings; in the form of cottage cheese (perhaps as a snack in celery sticks or as a dip with carrot sticks) or cheese (perhaps in sandwiches or in cubes, with apple). Milk will also supply over a quarter of the day's thiamin requirement. Nutritional yeast flakes, almonds, green vegetables, wheat germ, molasses, hummus, and tahini are other rich sources.

Thiamin and Niacin

A young child's needs for thiamin (see p. 22) can be met almost entirely by a 1-ounce serving of a fortified whole wheat breakfast cereal. Other sources of thiamin are whole wheat bread, legumes, Brazil nuts, dried fruit, and yeast extract, some or all of which will probably be eaten during the course of the day, so a standard vegetarian/vegan toddler diet presents no problem here. One alternative to the fortified breakfast cereal could be a mixture of $1/4$ cup of finely grated Brazil nuts, three chopped or pureed dates, and $1/2$ tablespoon (or more) wheat germ; this provides nearly six-sevenths of the daily thiamin needs and can be added to a few rolled oats for a muesli mix or to plain yogurt. Or, for older children, the dates can be stuffed with the Brazil nuts and the wheat germ can be added to something else during the day.

Niacin requirements (see p. 22) are a little more difficult to meet, so this is a nutrient that needs watching. Fortified breakfast cereals are a good source, and a 1-ounce serving of breakfast cereal, plus the milk and two slices of bread already suggested, will supply around 5.5 mg. Peanut butter, brewers' yeast (in the form of nutritional yeast flakes sprinkled over dishes), brown rice, and sunflower seeds are all rich in niacin.

Iron

Iron is another nutrient you need to keep your eye on. However, if your toddler has two slices of whole wheat bread a day, supplying 1 mg, plus an iron-enriched cereal, these together will supply around a fifth of her daily requirements. If your child is consuming $2^{1}/2$ cups of soy milk, that will supply another 3.6 mg.

Vitamins A, C and D

Vitamin C is unlikely to be a problem. The whole of the recommended daily allowance (see p. 10) can be supplied by 3–4 ounces of orange or grapefruit, two tangerines, a small glass of orange juice, or one large tomato, or by 3 ounces of strawberries.

These are all sources of vitamin A as well (see p. 10). And the recommended amount of milk supplies half the recommended daily allowance, as does half a pat of butter or margarine. Carrots are also an

CAUTIONARY NOTES ON FOODS FOR YOUNG BABIES

FOOD	REASON
Salt, and salty foods, including chips and savory snacks, salted stock, soy sauce, and yeast extracts (except low sodium)	Too much salt is not good for anyone; in babies under 18 months it can put excessive strain on (and even possibly damage) the liver and kidneys.
Spices, including curry powder, pepper, nutmeg, and mustard	Same as above.
Refined flour and flour products	Often contain additives, such as bleaching agents, preservatives, and so on, and may also contain traces of chemicals used in the growing process (fertilizers, pesticides), which can cause allergies. But 100% whole wheat flour and bread may be too high in fiber for some babies under 12 months (see p. 65).
Sugar, and food and drink containing this, such as syrups and jams (Raw turbinado sugar can be used sparingly from two years on)	Contains no nutrients, only calories. Because it lacks fiber, it is taken into the bloodstream too quickly, causing the body to produce large amounts of insulin. Over a prolonged period, this has been linked with the development of mature-onset diabetes. Raw turbinado sugar does contain some nutrients, such as iron, calcium, and B vitamins, but this, too, should be restricted because of the lack of fiber. Dried and fresh fruit, date puree, honey, natural fruit juices, and sugar-free preserves are a better source of sweetness in the diet.
Honey (small amounts of real organic honey can be used from 12 months on)	Another concentrated food, which is why it is not recommended for young babies. It does not contain fiber, so it has the same disadvantages as sugar, except that honey contains natural antibiotics and has been found to have healing properties.
Processed, canned, and packaged foods containing additives such as preservatives, emulsifiers, artificial flavorings, and colorings	Not recommended at any age, but especially not for babies because of the danger of allergic reactions. Some additives have been linked with hyperactivity and aggression in young children. Permissible ones, in my opinion, include canned beans, baked beans, and tomatoes.
Whole nuts, both salted and unsalted (Unsalted whole nuts can be given from about five or six years on)	They can get stuck in the baby's throat and cause choking. Salted nuts have the additional disadvantages described under Salt.
Caffeine (found in coffee, tea, cola drinks, chocolate, and products made from cocoa)	It is a stimulant.

FOOD	REASON
Alcohol	Because of their small body weight, the undesirable effects of alcohol are magnified if it is given to young children. Also in countries where it is normal to give young children diluted wine, this is being linked with alcoholism later in life.
Deep-fried foods	Fat is difficult for a baby to digest, and too much fat is undesirable in any diet. Heating certain types of oil to the temperatures required for deep frying alters the chemical structure, making it potentially harmful.
Skim milk, soy milk	A baby needs the extra fat and calories in whole milk. Skim, lowfat, and soy milk are too low in these. Use whole milk until your child is five years old (lowfat after two years in certain cases, under medical supervision) and soy formula milk until the age of five. If soy milk is used between two and five years, it is important that the lower energy content is compensated for by other foods as part of a well-balanced diet.
Eggs	Ensure that eggs are always thoroughly cooked to avoid the risk of salmonella. Boiled eggs, in particular, should always be cooked until both the yolk and white are solid.

excellent source of this vitamin, and just $1/2$ ounce of raw carrot will supply the entire day's recommended allowance of vitamin A.

Vitamin D can be more of a problem. A 1-ounce serving of fortified margarine supplies nearly a quarter of the RDA (see p. 83) and breakfast cereals fortified with vitamin D can also supply some, as can cheese, milk, eggs, and yogurt. For most children, however, a vitamin D supplement, in the form of drops, is a sensible precaution.

Many people worry about getting enough protein in a vegetarian diet. But as I explained on p. 4, a vegetarian diet that contains adequate amounts of calcium, iron, and B vitamins will automatically contain enough protein.

Putting it into Practise

To sum up, the following foods provide an excellent daily nutritional basis for your toddler:

- $2^1/2$ cups of whole milk or soy milk formula, or equivalent in cheese or yogurt
- 1 ounce vitamin-enriched breakfast cereal, or the equivalent described below
- two thick slices whole wheat bread
- $1/3$ cup orange juice or 3–4 ounces of orange
- Vitamin D and, if necessary, B12 supplement

To these you need to add, in particular, foods that are rich in iron. Children of this age can be extremely fussy, and some foods will be more readily accepted than others, so choose wisely. Some suggestions would be 1-2 daily servings of legumes, peanut butter, almonds, or pumpkin seeds; a serving of potato or grain such as brown rice, millet, whole wheat pasta or whole wheat bread (in addition to the above); dried fruit (including prune juice if liked); yeast extract; wheat germ; and as many raw and cooked vegetables (including a daily serving of leafy vegetables if possible) as your child will eat.

Here's how this scheme works out in terms of meals:

Menu Plans for the Vegetarian/Vegan Toddler

- Breakfast:
  Fortified whole wheat cereal with milk or soy milk, a sprinkling of wheat germ, nutritional yeast flakes and raisins; whole wheat toast with yeast extract; milk
  or rolled oats, flaked millet, and wheat germ soaked in prune juice with chopped dates and grated Brazil nuts; milk
  or chopped banana, wheat germ, grated Brazil nuts, chopped dates, yogurt; whole wheat toast with yeast extract; milk
  or cereal or oat mix as above; boiled egg with fingers of whole wheat bread or toast; milk
- Mid-morning and/or Mid-afternoon: Orange juice diluted with a little water

(or prune juice, if your toddler is getting enough vitamin C from other sources, see p. 10)

- Lunch and Dinner: (see opposite)

- Bedtime: Milk

In planning the menus opposite, I have allowed a legume dish either at lunch or dinner; a green vegetable either at lunch or dinner; bread, pasta, cereal, or potato at either or both; a fruit and milk dessert or its equivalent. Make sure that your toddler is getting $2^1/2$ cups of whole milk or soy milk formula during the day.

Eating Between Meals: Healthy Snacks

Snacks between meals are not necessarily a bad thing if they're nutritious. Indeed, they may be the most acceptable and harmonious way of getting nourishment into a difficult toddler! Here are some ideas for between-meal nibbles that contribute positively to the diet:

- Carrot sticks
- Celery sticks filled with cottage cheese, Hummus (p. 91), or Tahini Dip (p. 90)
- Fingers of whole wheat toast (or whole wheat rusks) with peanut butter, hummus, or tahini dip
- Figs, dates, raisins, and dried apricots
- Whole almonds, Brazil nuts, and pumpkin seeds (given under supervision, in case of choking, from around five years old)

ONE WEEK'S MENUS FOR YOUR TODDLER'S LUNCH AND DINNER
(Dishes marked * are suitable for freezing)

LUNCH	DINNER
Tofu Potato Cakes (p. 125) with Parsley Sauce* (p. 93) and carrot sticks Sections of orange Milk or soy milk	Whole wheat bread with peanut butter or Tahini Dip (p.90) and slices of tomato Grated apple with yogurt, raisins, and wheat germ Milk or soy milk
Leftover Broccoli and Corn Pie* (p. 130) with brown rice and slices of tomato Finely grated apple with a little yogurt and wheat germ Milk or soy milk	Hummus* (p. 91) with fingers of whole wheat toast Carrot sticks Millet and Raisin Cream (p.144) Milk or soy milk
Baked potato mashed with a little finely grated cheese or tofu and finely grated carrot Banana mashed with a little yogurt and grated pumpkin seeds Milk or soy milk	Very Quick Lentil Soup* (p. 101) and whole wheat roll Raw broccoli florets Ripe pear slices Milk or soy milk
Leftover Lentil Soup with whole wheat bread mashed into it Slices of tomato Fresh fruit prepared for finger-feeding Milk or soy milk	Hummus* (p. 91) with broccoli florets, carrot sticks, and whole wheat toast Slices of apple Milk or soy milk
Leftover Lentil and Broccoli Gratin* (p. 118), reheated and mashed with skinned tomato Soaked dried apricots pureed with yogurt, topped with sprinkling of wheat germ	Spicy Beanburger* (p. 127) with watercress and carrot sticks Muesli: yogurt mixed with rolled oats, wheatgerm, finely grated apple, raisins, powdered pumpkin seeds Milk or soy milk
Scrambled egg or Scrambled Tofu (p. 125) on crumbled whole wheat bread with shredded watercress Sections of orange	Red Kidney Bean and Avocado Salad (p. 99) with shredded lettuce and carrot sticks Fingers of whole wheat bread with yeast extract Slices of apple

- Molasses Oat Bars (p. 137)
- Fruit and Nut Bars (p. 140)
- Yogurt-and-fruit milk shakes
- Homemade yogurt or orange juice ice pops
- Nutty Carob Bananas (p. 139)
- Healthy Ice Cream (p. 150)
- Cubes of cheese

- Brown rice cakes (with no added salt) from the health food store

Survival Tips

- Do not worry if your child really does not like some food; you can usually find another source of the same nutrients. As I've said before, it's better to stick to foods you know will go down well – and avoid battles of will.

● All children go through a stage when they learn the power of the word no. If this veto is used over food, you may be able to nip it in the bud by offering a choice of two equally nutritious items instead of single suggestions they can refuse.

● Do not worry if your toddler eats foods in the "wrong" order or mixes things up (after all, that's part of the fun, spoil-sport!); and don't set too high a standard.

● If there's a problem over food, the secret is not to get emotional about it, either because you're worried about your toddler's health or because

it's hurtful to have your food refused. It simply isn't worth making an issue over food or allowing a difficult situation to develop. In fact, as always, it's your relationship with your child that's the most important thing. This is what you're building up and what will endure long after you've forgotten the horrors of broken nights, tantrums, food fads, and puddles on the carpet! Always put this relationship first, before a spotless house, before rigid timetables, before battles over food or anything else, and you will be rewarded by the deepening bond of understanding and companionship that will develop between you.

Nutrient Charts

REFERENCE DAILY DIETARY ALLOWANCES OF MAIN NUTRIENTS					
	AVERAGE MAN	AVERAGE WOMAN	PREGNANT WOMAN	LACTATING WOMAN	CHILD UP TO 3
Protein	63 g	50 g	+10 g	+15 g	16 g
Vitamin B1 (Thiamin)	1.5 mg	1.1 mg	+0.3 mg	+0.5 mg	0.7 mg
Vitamin B2 (Riboflavin)	1.7 mg	1.3 mg	+0.3 mg	+0.5 mg	0.8 mg
Niacin	19 mg	15 mg	+2 mg	+5 mg	9 mg
Vitamin B6 (Pyridoxine)	2 mg	1.6 mg	+0.6 mg	+0.5mg	1.0 mg
Folic Acid	200 mcg	180 mcg	+220 mcg	+100 mcg	50 mcg
Vitamin B12	2 mcg	2 mcg	+0.2 mcg	+0.6 mcg	0.7 mcg
Vitamin C	60 mg	60 mg	+10 mg	+35 mg	40 mg
Vitamin A	1000 mcg	800 mcg	no increment	+500 mcg	400 mcg
Vitamin D	5 mcg	5 mcg	+5 mcg	+5 mcg	10 mcg
Vitamin E	10 mg	8 mg	+2 mg	+4 mg	6 mg
Iron	10 mg	15 mg	+15 mg	no increment	10 mg
Calcium	800 mg	800 mg	+400 mg	+400 mg	800 mg
Magnesium	350 mg	280 mg	-20 mg	+75 mg	80 mg
Zinc	15 mg	12 mg	+3 mg	+7 mg	10 mg

SOME GOOD SOURCES OF NUTRIENTS IN THE VEGETARIAN/VEGAN DIET

Nutrient Content	Food	Amount of Food
PROTEIN:		
41.0 g	cottage cheese	10 ounces
13 g	yogurt	8 ounces
11.0 g	hard cheese	1 1/2 ounces
10.0 g	whole wheat pasta	2 ounces raw weight
12.7 g	cooked soybeans	4 ounces
7.57 g	sunflower, sesame, or pumpkin seeds	1 ounce
VITAMIN B1 (THIAMIN):		
2.4 mg	soy milk	1 cup
1.25 mg	brewers' yeast	1 tablespoon
0.6 mg	whole wheat pasta	2 ounces raw weight
0.35 mg	fortified wheatflakes	1 ounce
0.25 mg	yeast extract	1 teaspoon
0.2 mg	raw rolled oats	1 1/2 ounces
VITAMIN B2 (RIBOFLAVIN):		
0.79 mg	evaporated milk	1 cup
0.49 mg	yogurt	1 cup
0.42 mg	whole wheat pasta	2 ounces raw weight
0.42 mg	fortified wheatflakes	1 ounce
0.40 mg	milk	1 cup
0.34 mg	yeast extract	1 teaspoon
NIACIN:		
4.61 mg	roasted peanuts	1 ounce
4.6 mg	cooked brown rice	3 ounces
4.0 mg	raw whole wheat pasta	2 ounces
3.5 mg	fortified wheatflakes	1 ounce
3.0 mg	brewers' yeast	1 tablespoon
2.82 mg	dried apricots or peaches	4 ounces

Nutrient Content	Food	Amount of Food
VITAMIN B6 (PYRIDOXINE):		
0.68 mg	1 egg	2 ounces
0.47 mg	cooked corn	6 ounces
0.42 mg	1/2 avocado	3 1/2 ounces
0.41 mg	dried prunes	6 ounces
0.40 mg	1 banana	7 1/2 ounces
0.40 mg	1 medium-sized potato, baked in skin	7 1/2 ounces
FOLIC ACID:		
192 mcg	brewers' yeast	1 tablespoon
168 mcg	cooked lentils or beans	3 1/2 ounces
140 mcg	raw rolled oats	1 1/2 ounces
73 mcg	raw wheat germ	1 ounce
50-70 mcg	cooked broccoli or Brussels sprouts	5 ounces
42 mcg	2 slices whole wheat bread	1 1/2 ounces
VITAMIN B12:		
4.07 mcg	B12 fortified soy milk (check label)	1 cup
3.0 mcg	milk	1 cup
1.28 mcg	yogurt	1 cup
0.8 mcg	hard cheese	1 1/2 ounces
0.61 mcg	evaporated milk	1 cup
0.5 mcg	fortified breakfast cereal	1 ounce
VITAMIN C:		
140 mg	cooked broccoli	5 ounces
124 mg	orange juice	1 cup
102 mg	raw red bell pepper	2 ounces
88 mg	strawberries	5 ounces
66 mg	1 orange	6 ounces
38 mg	1/2 medium-size grapefruit	3 1/2 ounces

Nutrient Content	Food	Amount of Food
VITAMIN A:		
3836 RE	cooked sweet potato	4 ounces
2020 RE	1 large raw carrot	3 ounces
2416 RE	raw broccoli	5 ounces
1480 RE	dried apricots	4 ounces
962 RE	cooked kale	4½ ounces
855 RE	butter	4 ounces
VITAMIN D:		
6.52 mcg	evaporated milk	1 cup
2.24 mcg	margarine	1 ounce
0.75 mcg	1 egg	2 ounces
0.42 mcg	butter	1 ounce
0.11 mcg	milk	1 cup
0.08 mcg	hard cheese	1¹/₂ ounces
VITAMIN E:		
21.5 mg	wheat germ oil	1 tablespoon
11.0 mg	cold-pressed corn oil	1 tablespoon
3.15 mg	almonds	1 ounce
3.33 mg	wheat germ	1 ounce
1.0 mg	2 slices whole wheat bread	1¹/₂ ounces
1.0 mg	cooked Brussels sprouts	5 ounces
IRON:		
10.5 mg	prune juice	1 cup
5.0 mg	dried apricots	4 ounces

Nutrient Content	Food	Amount of Food
2.41 mg	dried prunes	4 ounces
5.4 mg	whole wheat pasta	2 ounces raw weight
4.0 mg	cooked spinach	6 ounces
2.93 mg	pumpkin seeds	1 ounce
CALCIUM:		
230 mg	yogurt	5 ounces
315 mg	hard cheese	1¹/₂ ounces
302 mg	milk	1 cup
135 mg	tahini	1 ounce
200 mg	cottage cheese	10 ounces
360 mg	cooked broccoli	8 ounces
MAGNESIUM:		
111 mg	1 piece tofu	3¹/₂ ounces
92.25 mg	raw millet	2 ounces
72 mg	almonds	1 ounce
66 mg	Brazil nuts	1 ounce
65 mg	sesame seeds	1 ounce
93.33 mg	raw wheat germ	1 ounce
ZINC:		
4.0 mg	raw wheat germ	1 ounce
2.02 mg	yogurt	1 cup
1.35 mg	Brazil nuts	1 ounce
1.6 mg	raw lentil sprouts	3¹/₂ ounces
1.58 mg	Gouda cheese	1¹/₂ ounces
1.25 mg	Cheddar cheese	1¹/₂ ounces
RE = *retinol equivalent*		

85

HOW IT ALL ADDS UP
(Analysis of One Day's Vegetarian Meals, Not Including Snacks)

Food	Calories	Fiber (in g)	Protein (in g)	Vit A (mcg)	B1 (mg)	B2 (mg)	B6 (mcg)	B12 (mcg)	Folic Acid (mcg)	Niacin (mg)	Vit C (mg)	Calcium (mg)	Iron (mg)	Magnesium (mg)	Zinc (mg)
4 slices whole wheat bread	342	1.6	4.8	tr	0.24	0.08	0.16	0	85	2.4	0	92	2	72	2
1 ounce butter (a)	204	0	0.1	940	tr	0.02		tr				6	0	tr	0.2
1½ ounces raw rolled oats	161	3	2.5	tr (b)	0.2	0.04	0.04	0	140	0.4	0	23	1.7	38	0.6
1 ounce wheat germ	82	0.75	7.3	0	0.55	0.22	0.25	0	73	1.16	0	20	2.55	93	4.0
1 ounce almonds	125	0.37	5.5	0	0.07	0	0.01	0	10	0.94	tr	62	1.28	72	0.75
1 ounce pumpkin seeds	116	9.2	7.57	15	0.05	0.04	0.16	0	22	0.51	0	13.5	2.92	35	
2 dried figs	107	7	2.2	32	0.05	0.03	0.15	0	15	0.8	0	63	1.5	32	
3½ ounces cooked lima beans	131	3.6	7.8	160	0.13	0.06		0	160 (c)	0.65	0	28	3		0.85
6 ounces cooked brown rice	178	1	8	0	0.14	0.3	0.3	0		9.2	0	18	0.8	90	0.8
3 tablespoons peanut butter	258	0	11.7	0	0.05	0.06	0.15	0	26	7.2	0	33	0.9	78	1.5
2 cups lowfat milk (d)	181		12.9	225	0.14	0.6	0.15	4.5	18	0.32	3	453	0.18	50	1.43
5 ounces Brussels sprouts	56	6.5	3.72	810	0.12	0.22	0.28	0	56	1.2	135	50	1.7	2	0.54
6 ounces orange	64	0.9	1.3	260	0.13	0.05	0.11	0	83	0.5	66	54	0.5	20	0.26
1 large (3½ ounces) raw carrot	42	3	1.1	1100	0.06	0.05	0.15			0.6	8	37	0.7	23	0.4
Total	2047	36.92	76.49	3542	1.93	1.77	1.91	4.5	688	25.88	212	952.50	19.73	605	13.33
RDA for Average Woman	2200	25	50	800	1.1	1.3	1.6	2	180	15	60	800	15	280	12

(a) Or vegetable margarine, which adds 2.5 mg of vitamin E.

(b) Unless fortified with this vitamin.

(c) Estimate.

(d) Or calcium-fortified soy milk. This increases the riboflavin a little and adds around 2 mg of iron, whilst supplying as much, or more, calcium (check your own brand).

Note: A blank means the information is not available.

PART II

RECIPES

All recipes marked * are suitable for freezing

DIPS & SAUCES

VINAIGRETTE

If you're making a bowl of salad, and everyone likes dressing, it's easiest
to mix it straight into the bowl, but if you want to add vinaigrette
individually it can be handy to have some made up in a jar ready for use.
Vary the proportions of oil and vinegar according to your own taste;
I prefer a simple, sharpish, not too oily vinaigrette.

**1 teaspoon sea salt
a grinding of black pepper
2 tablespoons red wine vinegar
6 tablespoons olive oil**

Put all the ingredients into a jar with a tight-fitting lid and shake well.

DATE SPREAD*

This is useful for sweetening yogurt and other puddings; also for
spreading on bread and butter or toast. Simply chop $^3/_4$ cup of cheapest
dried dates (not sugar-rolled) roughly, removing any pits or hard pieces.
Put the dates into a small saucepan with $^2/_3$ cup of water and heat gently
for 5-10 minutes, until soft. Beat to a puree with a wooden spoon and let
cool. This keeps for at least two weeks in a jar in the fridge.

NON-EGG MAYONNAISE

Useful if you want a homemade mayonnaise without any risk of
salmonella. This is much easier to make than real mayonnaise, tastes
good and will keep for up to a week in a jar in the fridge.

4 tablespoons soy milk
$1/4$ teaspoon powdered mustard
salt and freshly ground black pepper
$7/8$ cup light olive, grapeseed, or peanut oil
1 tablespoon lemon juice
1 tablespoon wine vinegar

Mix together the soy milk, powdered mustard and some seasoning. Then
gradually add the oil, a little at a time, whisking well after each addition.
When the mixture begins to thicken, you can add the rest more quickly,
in a thin, steady stream, but still whisking all the time. Then add the
lemon juice and vinegar and stir them in very gently in one direction
only, which will further thicken the mixture, because of the effect of the
acid on the milk. Check the seasoning – this mayonnaise needs plenty of
salt and pepper. Should the mayonnaise curdle, simply start again with 1
tablespoon soy milk in a clean bowl and whisk in the curdled mixture a
bit at a time. I did exactly that when I was testing this recipe, and it's fine!

GOMASIO

This highly nutritious Japanese seasoning, which is used instead of salt, is
excellent sprinkled over many savory dishes, steamed vegetables, grains,
salads, and as a dip for crudités. Put 10-12 teaspoons sesame seeds into a
dry skillet with 1 teaspoon sea salt. Stir over moderate heat for 1-2
minutes until the seeds "pop," smell roasted, and brown a little. Cool;
reduce to a powder in a coffee grinder or with a mortar and pestle. For
babies over a year old, use 20 teaspoons sesame seeds to 1 teaspoon salt.

YOGURT DIP/DRESSING

Simply mix chopped fresh herbs into unsweetened plain yogurt – soy or dairy – along with salt, pepper, and some crushed garlic to taste. Peeled, diced cucumber can also be added. Herbs which are especially good are mint, cilantro, flatleaf parsley, or chives.

TAHINI DIP/DRESSING

I warn you, this is addictive. The first time you taste it, it's a bit "er-um," but after another taste you'll be hooked on the intriguing flavor and creamy texture. Tahini dip makes an excellent topping for salads or filling for sandwiches. Packed with protein, iron, calcium, and B vitamins, it's particularly good for increasing your milk supply when you're breastfeeding – but it's good any time, for adults, babies, and children. You can make it thick, as a dressing or dip, to have with raw vegetables or strips of whole wheat pita bread; or thin, as a creamy, pouring sauce which is good with steamed vegetables.

SERVES 1

2 tablespoons pale tahini
1 garlic clove, peeled and minced
juice of $1/2$ lemon
salt and freshly ground black pepper

Put the tahini into a small bowl with the garlic, 1 teaspoon of the lemon juice, and 2 tablespoons water, and stir. The mixture will go very thick and lumpy to start with, then it will gradually become smooth and creamy. Add more water and lemon juice to get the consistency and flavor you want, and season with salt and pepper.

HUMMUS*

Although you can buy good hummus, it's easy to make your own, and worth it if you eat a lot of it. I generally use canned chick peas because they puree easily, although cooking your own reduces the cost even more and would be worthwhile if you wanted to make a really big batch. A 1-pound bag of chick peas produces the equivalent of five 16-ounce cans when soaked overnight and boiled until tender (which might take 2-3 hours). Hummus is great with salad, as a dip with raw vegetables or bread, or as a filling in sandwiches... Children love it once they get the taste for it, and it's extremely nourishing.

SERVES 2 ADULTS

16-ounce can chick peas or ²/₃ cup dried chick peas, cooked
2 garlic cloves, peeled
2 tablespoons pale tahini
1 tablespoon olive oil
juice of 1 lemon
salt and freshly ground black pepper

Drain the chick peas, saving the liquid. Then put the chick peas, garlic, tahini, olive oil, 2 tablespoons lemon juice, and 4 tablespoons of the chick pea liquid into a food processor or blender and blend until smooth. Season with salt and pepper, and taste. Add more lemon juice – I generally use it all – if you like, and more liquid if it's too thick. Check the seasoning again and serve.

TOMATO SALSA

Salsa is halfway between a salad and a sauce, and it's good with many spicy legume and grain dishes. You can add extra ingredients to the basic mixture, such as chopped cilantro, scallions, seeded and finely shredded green chilies, ground coriander, lemon zest, chopped avocado.

5-6 tomatoes, skinned and chopped
1 onion, peeled and chopped
1 garlic clove, peeled and minced
salt
lemon juice

Mix the tomatoes, onion, and garlic together in a bowl, and season with salt and a squeeze of lemon juice.

TOMATO SAUCE*

This sauce is so useful, it's worth making a double quantity for the freezer. To freeze, pour into a suitable covered container, allowing room for the sauce to expand as it freezes. To use, let thaw for about 2 hours, then stir gently over moderate heat.

MAKES ABOUT 1^1/$_2$ CUPS

1 onion, peeled and chopped
2 tablespoons oil
16-ounce can tomatoes
salt and pepper

Fry the onion in the oil for 10 minutes, until soft, then remove from the heat, add the tomatoes, and puree in a blender – no further cooking is needed. Season to taste with salt and pepper.

PARSLEY SAUCE*

I like to get unbleached white flour from the health food store for this sauce, as it's free from chemicals and additives, but ordinary all-purpose flour would also do. It's best to use either butter and milk or a pure vegetable margarine and soy milk. Make sure you add plenty of parsley for color and nutrients – it's a useful source of calcium and iron. To freeze, pour into a suitable covered container, allowing enough room for the sauce to expand as it freezes. To use, let thaw for about 2 hours, then stir gently over moderate heat.

MAKES ABOUT 2^1/$_2$ CUPS

4 tablespoons butter or pure vegetable margarine
^{1}/$_2$ cup unbleached white flour
2^1/$_2$ cups milk or soy milk
1 bay leaf
salt and pepper
at least 2 heaping tablespoons chopped parsley

Melt the butter or margarine, then stir in the flour. Cook for 1 minute, add a third of the milk and stir until thickened; repeat with another third; then add the rest, together with the bay leaf and seasoning. (Or put all the ingredients, except the parsley, into a saucepan and whisk together over moderate heat until thickened.) Once the sauce is cooked, add the parsley. Alternatively, puree the butter or margarine, flour, and milk in a blender for 1 minute, pour into a saucepan and stir over moderate heat until thickened. In all cases, simmer gently for 10 minutes, to cook the flour, season and add the parsley.

VARIATION
To make a Cheese Sauce, omit the parsley and stir 1 cup of grated cheese and a pinch of dry powdered mustard or cayenne pepper into the cooked sauce.

SALADS

A fresh, lively green salad goes with so many dishes and is an excellent way of getting your daily green vegetables. Just tear the leaves and mix them with a little Vinaigrette (p. 88), any fresh herbs that you have, and any other ingredients you fancy, such as scallions, capers, or sliced avocado.

A tomato salad works best if you slice the tomatoes (which needn't be peeled) 30-60 minutes beforehand. Put them into a shallow dish and drizzle a little vinaigrette over them. Tear some basil over, if you have some, or add some thinly sliced onion.

For a mixed Italian salad, make a base of torn green salad leaves, top with sliced tomato, cucumber, celery, or whatever is available, and some coarsely grated carrot. Spoon a little vinaigrette over the top.

Apart from these three basic salads, there are all sorts of variations you can try.
Here are a few suggestions.

EASTERN-STYLE SALAD WITH ARAME

Arame seaweed is sweet and delicious. It looks pretty in a salad made from diced cucumber, sliced radishes, fresh, frozen or canned corn, and chopped scallions. Prepare the arame (about $1/2$ ounce will be enough) by soaking it for 5 minutes in cold water, then simmering for 10 minutes; drain and let cool, then mix with the other ingredients. Dress with a little rice vinegar, or white wine vinegar, salt, pepper, and sugar.

INDIAN CARROT SALAD

Fry 2 teaspoons white or brown mustard seeds in 1 tablespoon peanut oil until they pop – this only takes a few seconds. Remove from the heat. Add this to coarsely grated carrot, along with some lemon juice and salt and pepper. Some poppy seeds can be added, too.

CRUDITÉS

I particularly like Middle Eastern-style crudités, which involve a minimum of preparation. You do need very fresh vegetables: whole, crisp scallions; chunks of cucumber and scraped carrot; thick pieces of red, green, or yellow bell pepper; sprigs of fresh mint, cilantro, and parsley; wedges of tomato, and maybe some juicy olives thrown in, too.

COUNTRY SALAD

This is a salad with man-appeal, and one that children like too.
It's based on potatoes, with grated vegetables and beans added. I usually
cook the potatoes, in their skins, while I'm preparing the other
ingredients and then serve the salad warm as a quick main course (great
for Saturday lunch), on its own, or with a dollop of Tahini Dip (p. 90),
avocado dip, or Hummus (p. 91), and extra bread for those who want it.
Any that's left will keep well in the fridge.

SERVES 4 ADULTS

8–12 ounces potatoes
2 tablespoons olive oil
1 tablespoon red wine vinegar
salt and freshly ground black pepper
2 large carrots, scraped
1-2 raw beets, peeled
a bunch of watercress
6 ounces cabbage
16 oz can red kidney beans, drained

First put some water into a saucepan and start heating it, ready for
the potatoes. Scrub the potatoes (don't peel them), then cut into
$^1/_2$-inch dice, and put them into the water. Let simmer while you
prepare the rest of the ingredients. Put the olive oil and vinegar into a
large bowl or salad bowl, add some salt and pepper, and mix to make
a dressing. Coarsely grate the carrots and beets – you can do this
on a box grater straight into the bowl. Shred the watercress and
cabbage and add to the bowl, along with the kidney beans. Drain the
potatoes, which will probably be done by now – they need to be just
tender, not too soft. Mix everything together well, check the
seasoning, and serve.

CHICK PEA, TOMATO, AND GREEN BELL PEPPER SALAD

This salad is rich in vitamins, especially vitamins A and C. Serve with a lettuce or watercress salad and some bread – warm focaccia or whole wheat pita. Some Tahini Dip (p. 90), Yogurt and Mint Dressing (p. 90), or Non-Egg Mayonnaise (p. 91) also goes well with it.

SERVES 2 ADULTS

2 teaspoons red wine vinegar
1-2 tablespoons olive oil
salt and freshly ground black pepper
16-ounce can chick peas, drained
1 large green bell pepper, cored, seeded, and thinly sliced
1-2 beefsteak tomatoes, cut into
$^1/_2$-inch pieces
fresh parsley, cilantro or mint (if available)
lemon wedges

Put the vinegar and oil into a bowl, season and mix to make a quick dressing. Then add the chick peas, green bell pepper, and tomatoes, and stir gently so that they are all coated with the dressing. If you have some fresh herbs, snip some on top, before serving with lemon wedges.

LENTIL, RED BELL PEPPER, AND SPINACH SALAD

This salad is loaded with iron and vitamin C. Tasty little Puy (French) lentils are great if you can get them. If not, the larger green lentils can be used, though they take a bit longer to cook. Serve this with light mashed potatoes made with olive oil and/or focaccia or multigrain bread.

SERVES 2 ADULTS

1 cup Puy (French) lentils
2 large red bell peppers
1 pound tender spinach leaves, washed
olive oil
2 garlic cloves, peeled and chopped
salt and freshly ground black pepper
1 lemon, cut into wedges

Wash and drain the lentils, put them into a saucepan, cover generously with cold water and bring to the boil, then let simmer gently for 25-30 minutes, or until tender. If you are using the green lentils, treat them in the same way but let cook for 45-50 minutes.

Meanwhile cut the bell peppers into quarters and place them, shiny-side up, close to a hot broiler for about 15 minutes, until the skin is charred and blistered. Let cool until you can handle them, then if you wish peel off the skin, which will come away easily, and remove any seeds or pieces of stem. Cut the peppers into strips.

Next cook the spinach; heat 1 tablespoon olive oil in a large saucepan and put in about a quarter of the spinach. Cook over high heat for a few seconds only, until it has wilted, then take it out of the saucepan and put into a bowl. Repeat the process with the rest of the spinach, adding a little more oil if necessary, although it doesn't need much. Finally add the garlic to the saucepan and cook that for a few seconds, until it is golden but not brown. Pour the garlic and oil over the spinach in the bowl, and mix, adding salt and pepper to taste.

Drain the lentils. Arrange the spinach, lentils, and pepper strips in a shallow dish or on individual plates, garnished with lemon wedges, and pour a little olive oil over at the table if you wish.

RED KIDNEY BEAN AND AVOCADO SALAD

You could broil the red bell pepper if you wish (as described on p. 98), but in this salad I prefer the crunchy texture of raw pepper contrasting with the creamy avocado and "mealy" beans.

SERVES 2

2 teaspoons red wine vinegar
1-2 tablespoons olive oil
salt and freshly ground black pepper
16-ounce can red kidney beans, drained
1 large red bell pepper, cored, seeded, and thinly sliced
1 ripe avocado, pit and skin removed, flesh cut into
1-inch pieces
juice of $^1/_2$ lemon
fresh parsley or cilantro (if available)

Put the vinegar and oil into a bowl with some salt and pepper and mix to make a quick dressing. Then add the red kidney beans and red bell pepper. Sprinkle the avocado with lemon juice, season with a little salt and pepper, and add to the bowl. Mix gently and check the seasoning. If you have some fresh parsley or cilantro, snip some on top before serving.

Hot Potato Salad with Peanut Dressing

This is one of those dishes that sound very strange but taste really good. It's a mixture of hot and cold, bland and spicy, and it is rich in protein too.

SERVES 4 ADULTS

$1/2$ cup unsweetened shredded coconut
2 slightly heaping tablespoons smooth peanut butter
2 garlic cloves, peeled and minced
1 tablespoon soy sauce
1 tablespoon medium or sweet sherry
1 tablespoon rice vinegar or white vinegar
salt
$1^1/2$ pounds potatoes, washed or peeled
1 head of lettuce
1 bunch of watercress
4 tomatoes
1 onion

Put the coconut in a bowl and cover with $2/3$ cup boiling water. Let stand for 20 minutes, then strain the liquid in a small saucepan, discarding the coconut. Add the peanut butter, garlic, soy sauce, sherry, and vinegar, and heat gently, stirring, until smooth. Season with salt and keep warm.

Cut the potatoes into $1/2$-inch dice, boil until just tender, and drain. Wash the lettuce, watercress, and tomatoes, and peel the onion. Cut the onion and tomatoes into thin slices. To serve, spoon the hot potatoes into the center of a serving dish (or individual plates) and arrange the lettuce, watercress, tomatoes, and onion around the edge. Spoon the peanut sauce over the potatoes and serve at once.

SOUPS

VERY QUICK LENTIL SOUP*

This nourishing, iron-rich soup can be frozen in small portions, without the topping, for babies and toddlers.

SERVES 4 ADULTS

**8 ounces split red lentils
2 large onions, peeled and roughly sliced
2 garlic cloves, peeled and chopped
juice of $^1/_2$ lemon
salt and freshly ground black pepper
olive oil
1 teaspoon ground cumin (optional)**

Put the lentils, one of the onions, and the garlic into a large saucepan with 4 cups of water. Bring to the boil, then let simmer for about 30 minutes, until the lentils are very tender and pale. Stir well to get a smooth texture. Then add some lemon juice (start with 1 tablespoon) and some salt and pepper until it tastes just right, and serve. If you want to make it spicier, fry the other onion in a little oil for about 10 minutes, until it's crisp and lightly browned; add the ground cumin and stir for a few seconds longer. Pour this mixture over the top of the soup just before you serve it.

GREEK SPLIT PEA SOUP*

This takes about 2 minutes to put together, followed by long, slow simmering – $1^1/2$ hours – to produce a thick, filling, and very nutritious soup. Serve it with some bread or salad sandwiches for a cheap, easy lunch or supper. The texture is fairly smooth so it's ideal for babies and toddlers, and very popular with them (but leave the raw onion topping off their portion).

SERVES 4 ADULTS

$1^1/2$ cups yellow split peas
1 large onion, sliced
olive oil
salt and pepper
juice of 1 lemon
1 red onion, chopped (optional)

Put the split peas into a large saucepan with the onion, 5 quarts water, and 1 tablespoon olive oil. Bring to a boil, then skim off the froth. Let simmer gently, uncovered, for $1^1/2$ hours, stirring from time to time towards the end to prevent it sticking. It will be thick, fairly smooth, and creamy-looking. Season with plenty of salt and pepper and add the lemon juice, a bit at a time, until it tastes right: I generally find it will take the whole lot. Top each portion with a little olive oil and some chopped red onion if you wish.

Spinach Soup⋆

A pretty, creamy soup which tastes good and is packed with iron and folic acid.

SERVES 4 ADULTS

**1 tablespoon olive oil or butter
1 onion, finely chopped
1 garlic clove, peeled and sliced
1 medium potato, peeled and cut into $^{1}/_{2}$-inch cubes
1 pound spinach, thoroughly washed
$^{2}/_{3}$ cup light cream, milk or soy milk
salt and freshly ground black pepper
grated nutmeg**

Heat the oil or butter in a large saucepan, then put in the onion, garlic, and potato; stir, cover, and cook gently for 5-10 minutes, until softening. Add the spinach, stir and cook until it begins to wilt, then pour in $1^{1}/_{4}$ cups of water. Bring to a boil, cover, and let simmer for about 15 minutes, or until all the vegetables are tender. Puree in a blender and return to the saucepan. Stir in the cream, milk, or soy milk, and more water if necessary, to get the right consistency. Season with salt, pepper, and nutmeg; reheat and serve.

CREAMY POTATO AND ONION SOUP*

This is a comforting, nutritious soup, ideal for cold winter days.

SERVES 4 ADULTS

4 onions, peeled and chopped
1 pound potatoes, peeled and cut into even-sized pieces
3 tablespoons butter or pure vegetable margarine
1 tablespoon olive oil
salt and freshly ground black pepper
grated nutmeg

Put a quarter of the onions into a large saucepan with the potatoes and 4 cups of water. Bring to a boil, then cover and let cook until the potatoes are completely tender. Meanwhile melt the butter or margarine and oil in another saucepan, put in the remaining onions, cover, and cook gently for about 15 minutes, or until they are very soft. Puree the potato mixture in a blender or food processor, then return it to the saucepan. Add the onions to the saucepan, together with their buttery juices. Season to taste with salt, pepper, and nutmeg, reheat gently, and serve.

VARIATION
To make an equally good Creamy Potato and Leek Soup, use only one onion, cooked with the potatoes as described. Clean and slice 1 pound of leeks and cook in the butter and oil in place of the remaining onions. They may take a little longer than 15 minutes to become completely tender. Add the leeks to the pureed potato mixture as described.

SANDWICHES & SNACKS

FILLED PITA BREADS

A filled pita bread makes a convenient and tasty lunch or snack. Slit one of the long edges of a piece of whole wheat pita bread, then warm the bread under the broiler, turning it over when one side is done. Fill with any of the salads in this book: the Country Salad (p. 96), Lentil, Red Bell Pepper, and Spinach Salad (p. 98), or Chick Pea, Tomato, and Green Bell Pepper Salad (p. 97) are all good and can be topped with some Tahini Dip (p. 90) for extra interest if you wish. Broiled or roasted vegetables (pp. 112 and 114), left over from another meal, also make a great filling and you can use up any left-over cooked rice, risotto or pasta at the same time. Add some salad, a few olives, and some Non-Egg Mayonnaise (p. 89) for a quick, tasty, and very nutritious meal. Or try these fillings:

FELAFEL WITH SALAD

If you have some Felafel (p. 126) in the freezer and some Tahini Dip (p. 90) or Hummus (p. 91) in the fridge, you will be able to make this very quickly. Warm through (in a microwave or under a broiler) some felafel – maybe 3-4 per pita bread. Meanwhile, coarsely shred some lettuce – romaine if you have it – and slice a tomato, maybe a little onion or scallion and cucumber. Warm the pita bread, then fill it with the felafel and salad, adding a few black olives, and topping with a spoonful of tahini or hummus.

EGGPLANT, CHILI, AND TAHINI

Eggplant cooks down quite a bit, so you need to allow a whole medium one to make a well-packed pita. Wash and slice the eggplant. Brush the slices with olive oil and lay them flat on a broiler pan; broil first on one side then on the other until they are browned and tender. Sprinkle the eggplant slices with salt, pepper, and some store-bought hot chili sauce. Meanwhile prepare the Tahini Dressing (p. 90), making it a bit thinner than the recipe says, so that it will pour easily. Warm the pita bread, then fill it with the eggplant and a couple of spoonfuls of the tahini dressing. Add some black olives if you like and serve with a lemon wedge.

BURGER IN A BUN

This is quick to make using a homemade Spicy Beanburger (p. 127) from the freezer or a bought vegeburger. Pan-fry the burger on both sides. Meanwhile split a burger bun in half and warm under the broiler. Wash a couple of lettuce leaves and make some onion and tomato slices. Put the salad and burger on the bottom half of the burger bun, top with any sauces or pickles that you like – Non-Egg Mayonnaise (p. 89), Tahini Dip (p. 90), mustard, ketchup, pickles – then press the other half of the bun on top and serve.

AVOCADO AND ALFALFA IN A BURGER BUN

A soft, whole wheat bun – called in my local supermarket (rather quaintly, I think) a 'salad bun' – makes a good container for some sliced ripe avocado and nutritious alfalfa sprouts if you can get (or sprout) some. Put a lettuce leaf on one half of the bun, add lots of sliced avocado, alfalfa sprouts, salt and pepper, another lettuce leaf, and the top of the bun. Press together. Some Tahini Dip (p. 90) or Non-Egg Mayonnaise (p. 89), spread on the bun, helps it all stick together.

FRIJOLES REFRITOS IN TACOS

Mexican tacos will keep very well in the cupboard and then
in the freezer once opened. Warm one through under the broiler, then
top with hot or cold Frijoles Refritos (p. 128), shredded lettuce,
sliced tomato and some sliced or mashed avocado. Roll up firmly
and eat immediately.

FOCACCIA WITH AVOCADO, LETTUCE, AND TOMATO

Cut a focaccia loaf in half lengthways. Peel and slice a ripe avocado,
wash a few lettuce leaves, and slice a beefsteak tomato. Put layers of
these ingredients on the bottom half of the loaf, season with salt
and pepper, then put the other piece of bread on top. Cut in half or
quarters. Some fresh basil or cilantro, or a few drops of hot chili sauce,
are also good in this.

HUMMUS, BLACK OLIVE, AND CILANTRO SANDWICHES

Spread whole wheat or multigrain bread generously with Hummus
(p. 91), top with some chopped black olives and some fresh cilantro
leaves; spread another slice of bread with hummus, then press this on top.

AVOCADO SALAD SANDWICHES

Mash a ripe avocado with a little lemon juice, salt, and pepper.
Spread whole wheat bread with this mixture, and add some shredded
lettuce and sliced tomato. Spread another slice of bread with more
avocado and press on top.

BRUSCHETTA WITH HUMMUS, TOMATO, AND OLIVES

Toast some whole wheat bread under the broiler, rub with a cut clove of garlic, and brush with olive oil. Top with sliced tomato, season, then pile with Hummus (p. 91). Add some black olives and a few leaves of fresh cilantro if you have it.

BRUSCHETTA WITH TAHINI DIP AND BROILED RED BELL PEPPER

First broil a red bell pepper – or if you are doing this for two people, you could use one red and one yellow pepper. Cut them into quarters and put under a hot broiler for about 15 minutes until the skin is charred and blistered; cool, remove the skin, and slice the pepper. Allowing 2 pieces of whole wheat bread per person, toast the bread under the broiler, then rub the surface with a cut clove of garlic, and brush with olive oil. Top with some Tahini Dip (p. 90) and slices of bell pepper. You could add one or two leaves of fresh cilantro if you wish.

GARLIC BREAD*

This ever-useful accompaniment to soups and salads is easy to make but, to save time, it can be assembled ready for baking and frozen. For a large baguette, mince 2-4 garlic cloves and mix with 6 tablespoons butter, pure vegetable margarine or olive oil. Make diagonal cuts in the loaf almost, but not quite, through to the base. Spread or brush the garlic mixture on the cut surfaces of the bread. Wrap suitably sized portions in aluminum foil and freeze, or bake immediately at 400°F for 20 minutes, or 30 minutes if baking them from frozen.

LEGUME & GRAIN DISHES

Legume and grain dishes provide the basis of a whole range of highly nutritious main meals. To make them even more satisfying and enjoyable, you may wish to serve them with some vegetable accompaniments.

For instance, you could try boiled potatoes mashed with olive oil, garlic, and some of the cooking liquid from the potatoes. The better the olive oil, the better the flavor. And if you like your mashed potatoes creamier, you could use milk, soy milk or a little cream instead of some or all of the cooking liquid. Other root vegetables, such as pumpkin, turnip, and rutabaga, also make excellent accompaniments, prepared in the same way.

As well as potatoes, root vegetables, and/or bread, you could accompany a legume or grain dish with a few steamed vegetables, such as green beans, broccoli, and carrots, perhaps dressed with a little lemon juice and olive oil.

MEDITERRANEAN BUTTER BEAN CASSEROLE*

As long as you remember to soak the beans the night before, this couldn't be simpler to make, and it's wonderfully warming and nutritious. Serve it as a simple main course with good bread. If there's any left over, it's excellent cold, with a squeeze of lemon, as a salad or a filling for pita bread. Or, on cold winter days, you can blend it and pour it back into the saucepan through a strainer for a smooth, creamy soup.

SERVES 4 ADULTS

1 pound butter beans, navy beans or other dried white beans
2 carrots, scraped and sliced
1-2 celery stalks, chopped
1 large onion, peeled and sliced
1 bay leaf
4 tablespoons olive oil
salt and freshly ground black pepper
freshly chopped parsley (optional)

Put the beans into a large pot, cover generously with cold water and let soak overnight. Next day, drain and rinse the beans, then put them back into the pot with the carrots, celery, onion, bay leaf, and olive oil. Bring to a boil – the liquid will foam, but give it a stir and it will soon subside. Let simmer, uncovered, for 2 hours, by which time the beans will be tender and the liquid will be thick and creamy. Season to taste with salt and pepper, and serve with chopped parsley on top, if you wish.

CHICK PEA STEW AND COUSCOUS*

SERVES 4 ADULTS

3 tablespoons olive oil
1 large onion, peeled and chopped
1 pound carrots, peeled and sliced
2 garlic cloves, peeled and minced
1 teaspoon ground ginger
$^1/_4$ teaspoon ground white pepper (if available)
$^1/_4$ teaspoon ground cinnamon
$^2/_3$ cup golden raisins
16-ounce can chick peas or $^2/_3$ cup
dried chick peas (soaked and cooked as described on p. 91)
8 ounces zucchini
salt
2 cups couscous
3 tablespoons butter
chopped flatleaf parsley

Heat 2 tablespoons oil in a large pot and put in the onion and carrots; cover and let cook gently for 10 minutes. Add the garlic and spices, stirring, and cook for 1-2 minutes, then add the golden raisins to the pot. Drain the chick peas (saving their liquid) and add to the pot. Make their liquid up to 4 cups with water and pour that in. Bring to a boil, then let simmer for about 20 minutes. Slice the zucchini, add to the pot, cover and let cook for another 10 minutes.

Meanwhile, prepare the couscous. Put the remaining tablespoon of oil into a large saucepan with $1^1/_2$ cups of water and $1^1/_2$ teaspoons salt and bring to a boil. Sprinkle in the couscous, take off the heat and let sit for 2 minutes. Then add the butter, put the saucepan back on the stove and heat gently, stirring with a fork, for 3 minutes. Check the seasoning of the stew, sprinkle with the parsley, and serve with the couscous.

BULGUR OR BUCKWHEAT WITH BROILED VEGETABLES

You need a wide broiler for this to make room for all the vegetables. If you haven't got a big broiler, either do them in two batches – they can be served warm rather than hot – or use the oven and roast them (as described on p. 114).

SERVES 3 ADULTS

1 fennel bulb, if available (otherwise use an extra onion)
1-2 onions, preferably red, peeled and cut into chunks
1 medium eggplant, cut into 1-inch chunks
2 medium zucchini, cut into 1-inch chunks
1 red bell pepper, seeded and cut into 1-inch squares
1 yellow bell pepper, seeded and cut into 1-inch squares
2 garlic cloves, peeled and chopped
4 tablespoons olive oil
salt and freshly ground black pepper
1^1/$_3$ cups bulgur or unroasted buckwheat groats
a little fresh basil, cilantro or flatleaf parsley

Set the broiler to high. Half-fill a medium saucepan with water and put on the stove to heat. Trim any green leaves from the fennel and keep for garnishing, then trim the root end. Cut the fennel in half, then cut each half into sixths or eighths. Put the fennel into the boiling water and simmer for 4 minutes, until just tender, then drain. (The liquid makes good vegetable stock.) Put the fennel into a bowl with all the other vegetables and sprinkle 3 tablespoons olive oil on top. Mix with your hands, or with a spoon, so that all the vegetables are coated with the oil, and put them into a broiler pan or a flat shallow baking pan that will fit under your broiler. Season with salt and pepper, then broil for 20 minutes, until all the vegetables are tender and flecked with brown, turning the heat down a bit after 10 minutes.

Meanwhile rinse the bulgur or buckwheat quickly in a strainer. Heat 1 tablespoon of oil in a saucepan, add the grains, and stir for 1-2 minutes, until most of the water has been absorbed. Remove from the heat and let sit for 5 minutes. Fluff with a fork. Check the seasoning, then make a bed of bulgur or buckwheat on a large plate, pile the vegetables in the middle, and serve with fresh basil, cilantro, or flatleaf parsley torn over the top.

MICROWAVE RISOTTO*

It's blissfully easy to make a wonderful risotto in the microwave. This method was developed by the cookery writer, Barbara Kafka.

SERVES 2-3 ADULTS

2 tablespoons butter
2 tablespoons olive oil
1 onion, peeled and chopped
3 garlic cloves, peeled and minced
1 cup arborio rice
2 ounces fresh Parmesan cheese
salt and freshly ground black pepper

Put the butter and oil into a deep, non-metal microwave-proof dish. (At every stage, keep the dish uncovered and microwave on high.) Put into the microwave and microwave for 2 minutes. Add the onion and garlic and stir to coat in the butter and oil. Microwave for 4 minutes. Add the rice, stir, then microwave for 4 minutes. Pour in 3 cups of boiling water. Microwave for 9 minutes. Stir well, then microwave for 9 minutes more.

Remove from the oven. Let the risotto sit, uncovered, for 5 minutes, to let the rice absorb the rest of the liquid, stirring several times. Flake the Parmesan with a vegetable parer or sharp knife, then stir this in, together with salt and pepper to taste, and serve.

ROASTED VEGETABLES WITH OVEN-BAKED RICE

A mixture of brown and wild rice makes a flavorful accompaniment for roasted vegetables, though you could use just brown rice for a cheaper version. Some roasted nuts and seeds – pumpkin, sunflower, almond, pistachio – are a nutritious addition to the rice; add just before you serve it.

SERVES 4 ADULTS

$1^1/_4$ cups brown rice
$^1/_4$ cup wild rice
1 onion, peeled and chopped
salt
12 ounces celery root
12 ounces parsnips
12 ounces rutabaga
12 ounces red onions
3 tablespoons olive oil
1 head of garlic

Set the oven to 400°F. Wash the rice (both types together if you are using the wild rice) in a strainer under cold running water. Then put them into a casserole dish with the onion, some salt, and 2 cups of boiling water. Cover and put near the bottom of the oven – it doesn't matter if it hasn't got up to full temperature by this time.

Next, put a large pot of water on the stove. Peel the celery root, parsnips, and rutabaga, then cut them into chunks. Trim the top of the red onions and peel off the outer skin without removing the root; then cut them into quarters, still leaving the root, which will hold them together. Put the olive oil into a roasting pan and put it in the oven to heat up; meanwhile put the vegetables into the pot of water and boil them for 5 minutes. Drain the vegetables, put them into the sizzling hot fat and place in the oven.

Meanwhile, break the garlic into cloves but don't peel them. Add the garlic to the vegetables after they have been roasting for about 15 minutes, then roast them for a further 15-20 minutes, or until they are golden brown. Cook the rice while the vegetables are roasting. Fork through the rice and serve with the vegetables.

OVEN-BAKED LEEK AND SUN-DRIED TOMATO RISOTTO*

Cooked in the oven instead of on top of the stove, this is another easy way to make a risotto. You really need risotto rice such as arborio to get the traditional creamy effect. If you want to try it with brown rice, get the short-grain 'pudding' type from the health food store and bake for 50 minutes instead of 35 minutes.

SERVES 2 ADULTS

8 ounces leeks, cleaned and sliced
1 onion, peeled and chopped
4 tablespoons butter
1 cup risotto rice
6 sun-dried tomatoes, chopped
salt and freshly ground black pepper
a wine glass of sherry, Madeira
or white wine
a few flakes of fresh Parmesan cheese (optional)

Set the oven to 300°F. Fry the leeks and onion in the butter, gently, covered, for 20 minutes. Add the rice, sun-dried tomatoes, 1 teaspoon salt, some pepper, the sherry, Madeira or white wine and $2^1/_2$ cups water. Transfer to a shallow gratin dish. Bake, uncovered, for 20 minutes, then stir. Return to the oven for a further 15 minutes; stir and serve, with the Parmesan cheese if using.

PARSLEY AND ONION POLENTA*

Once made, polenta can be cut into pieces and broiled, baked, or fried. It will keep in the fridge for a few days before cooking, or for up to six months in the freezer, and can be cooked from frozen. In the summer it is excellent with asparagus – which can be oven-baked too – and you can also grill it over a barbecue. A Tomato Sauce (p. 92) or Salsa (p. 92) goes well with it.

SERVES 4 ADULTS

**2 cups coarse cornmeal
olive oil
1-2 onions, peeled and chopped
2 garlic cloves, peeled and minced
2-3 tablespoons chopped parsley (flatleaf if possible)
salt and freshly ground black pepper
lemon wedges**

Put the cornmeal into a medium saucepan and mix to a smooth paste with 4 cups of cold water. Then put the saucepan on the heat and stir gently until the mixture comes to a boil and is thick and smooth. Let the polenta cook gently until it is very thick and comes away from the sides of the saucepan – about 30 minutes. (Make sure you cook it for long enough, otherwise it won't set.) Meanwhile heat 1 tablespoon olive oil in a saucepan, put in the onion and garlic, cover, and cook for 10 minutes. When the polenta has cooked, stir in the parsley and season with plenty of salt and pepper. Spread the mixture out on an oiled flat plate, baking pan, or cookie sheet, to a depth of just under $^1/2$ inch, then let cool.

Just before you want to serve the polenta, cut it into slices. To fry: heat a little olive oil in a skillet and put in the slices; fry until they are crisp and golden on one side, then turn them over and fry the other side in the same way. Drain on paper towels. To broil: brush the polenta slices on both sides with olive oil, place under a broiler until the top is flecked with brown, then turn over to do the other side. To bake: brush the polenta slices with oil as before, place on a cookie sheet and bake near the top of a moderate to hot oven, say 400°F, for 30-40 minutes, turning them over after about 20 minutes. Serve with lemon wedges and your chosen accompaniment.

VARIATION

Make as above but replace the parsley with $2/3$ cup pitted olives: green or black or a mixture. A tomato sauce goes particularly well with this tangy version.

LENTIL AND BROCCOLI GRATIN*

Based on one of my earliest and most popular recipes from *Not Just a Load of Old Lentils*, this is a good way of eating green vegetables, freezes well, and only needs a little salad – or a baked potato – to accompany it.

SERVES 4 ADULTS

1 cup red split lentils
4 tablespoons olive oil
1 large onion, peeled and chopped
1-inch piece of fresh ginger, peeled and grated
12 ounces broccoli, washed, trimmed, divided into florets
juice and grated rind of 1 lemon
salt and freshly ground black pepper
soft bread crumbs
grated cheese (optional)

Put the lentils into a saucepan with $2^1/_2$ cups of water, bring to a boil, then let simmer for 20-30 minutes, until they are soft and pale. Meanwhile, heat half the oil in a saucepan, add the onion and ginger, and cook for 10 minutes, uncovered, so that they brown a bit, stirring from time to time.

Steam the broccoli until it is just tender, then put it in a shallow gratin dish. Put the lentils into a food processor or blender, with the onion mixture and the lemon, and blend to a smooth puree.
It should be the consistency of heavy cream; add some water or milk if it is too thick. Season, then pour this puree evenly over the broccoli. Sprinkle the bread crumbs and remaining oil on top, or the crumbs and cheese (if you use the cheese, you won't need the extra oil).
Put under a moderately hot broiler for about 20 minutes, until the top is brown and the inside piping hot. Alternatively, bake at 350-400°F for 30-40 minutes.

Spinach Dal*

This comes from my book *The Classic Vegetarian* and is packed with iron.
Serve it with brown rice and a Tomato and Cilantro Salsa (p. 92).

SERVES 2-4 ADULTS

2 tablespoons peanut oil
2 onions, peeled and finely chopped
1 green chili
2 garlic cloves, peeled and minced
2 teaspoons ground cumin
$1/4$ teaspoon ground turmeric
3-4 cardamom pods
$2/3$ cup red lentils
1 pound spinach
salt and freshly ground black pepper

Heat the oil in a large saucepan, add the onions, and cook gently, covered,
for 10 minutes. Meanwhile halve the chili and scoop out the seeds, then slice
the chili. (Avoid touching your face while you are preparing the chili, and
wash your hands afterwards – the strong juice can burn your skin.) Add the
chili to the onion, along with the garlic, cumin, and turmeric. Crush the
cardamom pods, and add to the saucepan. Stir and let cook for a moment
or two, then add the lentils and pour in 2 cups of water. Bring to a boil,
cover, and simmer gently for 20-30 minutes, or until the lentils are very soft.

When the lentils are nearly done, wash the spinach thoroughly in 2-3
changes of water and remove any tough stems. Put the spinach into a dry
saucepan and cook over moderately high heat until the leaves have wilted
and the spinach is tender and much reduced in size – about 7 minutes.
Drain well in a colander. Add the spinach to the lentils, mixing well and
seasoning with salt and pepper. Serve the dal at once or reheat when
needed; it's also very good the next day.

CREAMY CASHEW NUT KORMA*

Creamy and lightly spiced, this is based on a recipe in my book *Vegetarian Fast Food*. It's delicious with rice and Indian breads.

SERVES 4 ADULTS

$^2/_3$ cup unsweetened shredded coconut
2 tablespoons peanut oil
2 onions, peeled and chopped
2 chilies
2 garlic cloves, peeled and minced
$^1/_2$ teaspoon ground cumin
$^1/_2$ teaspoon ground turmeric
$^1/_2$ teaspoon ground coriander
1 cup cashew pieces
salt and freshly ground black pepper
8 ounces broccoli, washed, trimmed, and divided into small florets
6 ounces green beans, trimmed, halved if long
1 cup frozen peas
2-4 tablespoons chopped fresh cilantro

Put the coconut into a bowl and cover with 2 cups of boiling water; stir, and let sit for 20 minutes. Meanwhile heat the oil in a large saucepan, then put in the onion; cover, and let cook over gentle heat for 7 minutes. While the onion is cooking, halve the chilies, remove the seeds, then slice the chilies finely and add to the saucepan, along with the garlic. (Keep your hands away from your face while preparing the chilies, and wash them well afterwards because the juice can burn your skin.) Add the spices to the saucepan, stir well, and cook for a further 1-2 minutes.

Strain the coconut liquid, discarding the solids. If you have a food processor or blender, whizz the cashews to a smooth, creamy consistency with the coconut liquid; or, grind the cashews as finely as you can (an

electric coffee grinder does this well, in small batches), then mix with the coconut liquid. Either way, add this mixture to the saucepan; season with salt and pepper, cover, and remove from the heat.

Cook the broccoli and green beans in a large covered saucepan containing $1/2$ inch of boiling water, to half-boil, half-steam them, until they are only just tender. Keep them well on the crisp side as they will cook a bit more when they are added to the korma. Drain the vegetables, then stir them gently into the creamy cashew mixture, along with the frozen peas. Cook over gentle heat until the korma is hot. Check the seasoning, sprinkle with the cilantro, and serve.

SPICED VEGETABLE PILAU

I like this with something fresh – Tomato and Cilantro Salsa (p. 92) for instance – and poppadums and mango chutney.

SERVES 3 ADULTS

1 onion, peeled and chopped
1 garlic clove, peeled and minced
1 tablespoon peanut oil
$1/4$ teaspoon ground turmeric
$1/2$ teaspoon each of cumin seed, coriander seed, and fenugreek
$1\,1/4$ cups brown basmati rice
1 carrot, scraped and sliced
1 leek, washed and sliced
salt and freshly ground black pepper
$1/2$ cup roasted cashew pieces or shelled pistachios (optional)
chopped fresh cilantro (if available)

Cook the onion and garlic in the oil in a large saucepan, covered, for 5 minutes. Then add the turmeric, cumin, coriander, and fenugreek and stir over the heat for a few seconds until they smell aromatic. Wash the rice in a strainer under cold running water, drain, and add to the saucepan; stir for 1-2 minutes over the heat. Then add $1^1/2$ cups of boiling water. When the mixture comes back to a boil, cover, and leave over low heat for 5 minutes. Then, without disturbing the rice at all, uncover the saucepan and put the carrot and leek on top. Cover again and cook for a further 20 minutes. Remove from the heat and, if all the water hasn't been absorbed, just let sit for a further 5 minutes. Then fork the rice gently, adding some salt and pepper to taste. If using the nuts, add them to the mixture just before you serve it, with some chopped fresh cilantro on top if you have it.

Vegetable Stir-Fry with Tofu

A quick main course which is packed with B vitamins.

SERVES 2 ADULTS

8 ounces mushrooms
$^1/_2$ an onion or 3-4 scallions
8 ounces broccoli or snow peas, baby corn, or any other
suitable vegetable
peanut oil
10 ounces firm tofu, drained
1-inch piece fresh ginger, grated
1 garlic clove, peeled and minced
1 teaspoon cornstarch
1 tablespoon soy sauce
1 tablespoon sherry
$^1/_2$ cup cashew pieces (optional)
salt and freshly ground black pepper

Wash and slice the mushrooms; chop the onion or scallions and broccoli; trim the sugar peas if using. Fill a medium saucepan one-third full with peanut oil and heat. Meanwhile, cut the tofu into cubes and blot them on paper towels. When the oil is hot enough to form bubbles around a chopstick, drop in the tofu, in one layer. Deep-fry, drain on paper towels, and keep warm. You may need to do them in two batches.

Now heat 2 tablespoons oil in a large saucepan or wok. When it's smoking hot, put in all the vegetables, the ginger, and garlic, and stir-fry for 2-3 minutes until everything is heated through and beginning to get tender but still quite crunchy. Combine the cornstarch with the soy sauce and sherry and pour in. Stir for 1-2 minutes until thickened, then add the tofu, and the cashews if using. Stir gently for 1 minute, season with salt and pepper, and serve with boiled rice.

TOFU SATAY

A way of serving tofu that is really delicious. You need to allow 2 hours for the tofu to soak up the marinade but the recipe itself is very easy. Serve with boiled rice and an Oriental-style salad, steamed carrots (cut diagonally into oval slices) or snow peas.

SERVES 2 ADULTS

10 ounces firm tofu, drained and cubed
3 garlic cloves, peeled
2 tablespoons soy sauce
2 tablespoons medium or sweet sherry
1 tablespoon rice vinegar or white vinegar
$1/4$ cup unsweetened shredded coconut
2 slightly heaping tablespoons smooth peanut butter
salt

Put the tofu on a shallow plate. Mince 1 clove of garlic, mix together with the soy sauce, sherry and vinegar, and pour over the tofu. Stir gently, then leave for at least 2 hours. Heat the oven to 400°F.

Drain the tofu, saving the marinade. Put the tofu on a cookie sheet in a single layer and roast in the top of the oven for 25-30 minutes, until it is well-browned and fairly crisp.

Meanwhile make the sauce. Put the coconut into a bowl, pour over $2/3$ cup of boiling water and let sit for 20 minutes, then drain, discarding the solids. Mince the remaining garlic and put into a small saucepan with the coconut liquid, peanut butter, and the marinade. Heat gently, stirring, until smooth. Season with salt, and serve the tofu with the sauce.

TOFU POTATO CAKES

Young children love potato cakes and by mixing the potato with some tofu you can make them into a really nutritious meal. These are best made fresh, since tofu doesn't freeze well. Parsley Sauce (p. 93) goes well with them, and some sliced tomato.

MAKES 4 POTATO CAKES

9 ounces potatoes, peeled and cut into even-sized chunks
1 tablespoon butter or pure vegetable margarine
a little milk or soy milk
4 ounces firm tofu
1-2 tablespoons chopped parsley
salt and freshly ground black pepper
flour
peanut oil

Boil the potatoes until tender, then drain and mash with the butter or margarine and a little milk or soy milk if necessary. Mash the tofu, then add to the potato, along with the parsley and salt and pepper to taste. Form the mixture into four flat cakes, coat with flour, then either brush with oil and broil on both sides or pan-fry. Drain on paper towels.

SCRAMBLED TOFU

This is made with soft tofu, using the same method as you would use to make scrambled eggs. Simply melt a little vegetable margarine in a skillet, add some soft tofu and stir over moderate heat for 2-3 minutes. You can add a pinch of turmeric to give the tofu a yellow color, and salt and pepper to taste.

FELAFEL*

This is the traditional Israeli recipe for these crisp, tasty rissoles. If you like them, it might be worth making double the quantity, as I do, and freezing them. They only need reheating under a broiler or in a microwave and they make useful quick snacks with pita bread, salad, Hummus (p. 91), Tahini Dip (p. 90), and so on. You do need a food processor with a good sharp blade to make felafel – then it's surprisingly easy.

MAKES ABOUT 22 FELAFEL

**9 ounces dried chick peas
1 cup fresh parsley, thick stalks removed
1 garlic clove, peeled and roughly sliced
1 onion, peeled and cut into chunks
1 teaspoon each of ground coriander, ground cumin, and sea salt
peanut oil**

Put the chick peas into a large bowl and cover generously with cold water. Let soak for 24 hours. Drain and rinse the chick peas. Put them into your food processor with the parsley, garlic, onion, spices, and salt, then blend to a grainy paste which holds together. If it's on the wet side, chill in the fridge for an hour or so.

Heat the oil in a large saucepan until it forms bubbles around the end of a chopstick dipped into it. Form walnut-sized pieces of the mixture into balls, then flatten them a bit. Add them to the oil, three or four at a time. Fry for 2-3 minutes, until crisp and brown on the outside, then drain on paper towels.

Use immediately, or freeze by putting the cooled felafel on a cookie sheet and freezing until firm, then putting them into a plastic bag or container. To use, microwave or broil them straight from the freezer.

Spicy Beanburgers*

These are very popular with adults and children alike (though you may prefer to omit the chili powder when making them for toddlers). They freeze well and can be cooked from frozen.

MAKES 8 BURGERS

olive oil
1 onion, peeled and chopped
1 carrot, finely chopped or grated
$^1/_2$ green bell pepper, seeded and chopped
1 garlic clove, peeled and minced
$^1/_4$ - $^1/_2$ teaspoon hot chili powder (optional)
1 teaspoon ground coriander
2 sixteen-ounce cans red kidney beans
1 cup fresh whole wheat bread crumbs
salt and freshly ground black pepper
2 cups dry whole wheat bread crumbs

Set the oven to 400°F. Heat 1 tablespoon oil in a large saucepan, add the onion, and stir. Cover and let cook over moderate heat for 5 minutes, stirring occasionally. Then add the carrot, bell pepper, and garlic and cook for a further 5 minutes. Add the spices, stir for 1-2 minutes, then remove from the heat.

Mash the beans and add to the onion mixture, together with the fresh bread crumbs and seasoning to taste. Mash the mixture together very well at this stage because it's this which holds it together.
Divide into eight, form into burgers and coat with the dry crumbs. Place on an oiled cookie sheet and bake until brown and crisp on one side, then turn over to cook the other side.
Drain on paper towels and serve hot or warm.

FRIJOLES REFRITOS*

These are good with a salad, some tortilla chips, and sliced avocado; or as a filling for tacos (see p. 107). Sometimes I spice the flavor up with a bit of chili powder; add this when the onion is done and cook for a few seconds before starting to add the beans.

SERVES 4 ADULTS

1 onion, peeled and chopped
1 garlic clove, peeled and minced
2 tablespoons olive oil
2 sixteen-ounce cans red kidney beans
salt and freshly ground black pepper
chopped cilantro or grated cheese

Fry the onion and garlic in the oil in a fairly large saucepan for 10 minutes, until it is soft and lightly browned. Meanwhile drain the beans, saving the liquid. Add the beans to the saucepan a few at a time, mashing them as you do so. Continue in this way until all the beans have been used, adding a little of the reserved liquid if the mixture gets too dry. You can make the texture to suit your taste and even finish by pureeing some or all of it in a food processor if you want a smoother result. Then either scatter with chopped cilantro and serve, or put the mixture into a shallow dish, cover the top with grated cheese, and place under a broiler until it's golden brown and bubbly.

PIES, PIZZAS, & PASTA DISHES

PIE DOUGH*

Pie dough is not nearly as difficult to make as many people imagine, especially if you have a food processor.

MAKES TWO 8-INCH PIE SHELLS OR ONE 12-INCH PIE SHELL

2 cups flour, half whole wheat, half white
¹/₂ teaspoon salt
10 tablespoons butter or pure vegetable margarine

Put the flour into a food processor with a pinch of salt, then add the butter, cut into pieces, or margarine if using. Blend briefly until it looks like lumpy bread crumbs, then add 3 tablespoons water and blend, very briefly, until a ball of dough is formed. Remove from the food processor and, if you have time, cover and chill it in the fridge for 30 minutes. It can be frozen at this stage, or rolled out and pressed into a pie pan or pans.

Prick the pie shells lightly, then either freeze or bake at 400°F. Put a piece of wax paper in the pie shell with a few crusts of bread or dry beans on top to prevent it rising up. Bake for 10 minutes, then remove the paper and crusts or beans and bake until the base is crisp and golden brown – about another 15 minutes. Remove from the oven, put in your chosen filling, and return to the oven to heat through.

129

PIE FILLINGS

Quantities are for 8-inch pie shells. For a 10-inch pie shell, use one and a half times the amount; for a 12-inch pie shell, use double.

BROCCOLI AND CORN

12 ounces broccoli, washed and divided into florets
2 tablespoons butter or pure vegetable margarine
scant $^1/_4$ cup all-purpose flour
1$^1/_4$ cups milk or soy milk
1 cup frozen or drained canned corn
salt and freshly ground pepper
grated cheese (optional)

Steam the broccoli until just tender. Melt the butter or margarine in a saucepan, then add the flour. Stir over the heat for a few seconds until it froths. Pour in a third of the milk or soy milk. Stir over the heat until it thickens, then put in another third and repeat until it is all in. Stir until smooth, then cook over very gentle heat for 5-7 minutes to cook the flour. Add the drained broccoli and corn to the sauce. Season, spoon into the cooked pie shell, top with some grated cheese if you like, and place in the oven for 10-15 minutes to make sure everything is hot.

ONION AND OLIVE

2 tablespoons olive oil
1$^1/_2$ pounds onions, peeled and finely sliced
1 teaspoon white or light brown sugar
salt and freshly ground black pepper
$^1/_4$–1 cup black olives
grated cheese (optional)

Heat the oil in a large saucepan, then put in the onions. Cover and cook over gentle heat for 20-30 minutes, or until very soft. Add the sugar, turn up the heat, and cook for a few more minutes, until the onions have browned a bit. Season with salt and plenty of pepper, then stir in the black olives. Spoon the mixture into the pie shell, cover with grated cheese if you wish, and place in the oven for 10-15 minutes until the filling is piping hot and the cheese, if used, has melted and browned.

LEEK AND POTATO
2 tablespoons olive oil
1 pound leeks, washed and sliced
9 ounces potatoes, peeled and cut into $^1/_2$-inch chunks
2-3 tablespoons heavy cream or soy cream
salt and freshly ground black pepper
grated nutmeg
chopped parsley

Heat the oil in a saucepan and put in the leeks and potatoes. Cover and cook gently for 15-20 minutes, or until tender. Stir in the heavy cream or soy cream, and season to taste with salt, pepper, and grated nutmeg. Spoon into a hot pie shell, top with chopped parsley, and serve.

MUSHROOM
2 tablespoons butter or pure vegetable margarine
$1^1/_4$ pounds white mushrooms, washed, dried, and quartered
1 garlic clove, peeled and minced
1 teaspoon cornstarch
$^2/_3$ cup heavy cream
salt and freshly ground black pepper
grated nutmeg

Melt the butter or margarine in a saucepan and put in the mushrooms. Sauté over moderate heat for about 10 minutes until the mushrooms are tender and the liquid which they produce has boiled away. Add the garlic and stir over the heat. Mix the cornstarch with the cream, then pour this into the mushrooms, stirring over the heat until it has thickened – this will only take 1-2 minutes. Season with salt, pepper, and freshly grated nutmeg. Spoon into a hot pie shell and serve straight away.

Easy Yeast Pizza*

Making your own pizzas may seem unnecessary when you can buy them everywhere, but nothing beats a homemade one, with its thin, crisp base and luscious topping of your own favorite ingredients. It's much easier than you might think, and fills your home with the most inviting of baking smells. Once you have made the dough, it will keep in the fridge for a couple of days, or it can be frozen for 4-6 weeks. Then all you have to do is take a chunk of dough, roll it out thinly, put on your chosen topping, which can be as simple as you like, and bake it for 10-15 minutes. This recipe is based on one which appeared in my book
The Green Age Diet.
If you really don't have time to make your own, you can buy a very good ready-mix base. If you roll it out a bit thinner than it says on the packet, it will come out of the oven nice and crisp.

MAKES FOUR 12-INCH PIZZAS

3^1/$_2$ cups whole wheat or brown bread flour
^{1}/$_2$ teaspoon salt
1 packet instant yeast
olive oil

Put the flour, salt and yeast into a bowl. Add 1^1/$_4$ cups of tepid water. Mix to a dough which leaves the sides of the bowl clean, then turn out onto a clean work surface and knead until the dough feels smooth and silky. (Counting seems to make it easier: 200 times is about right, and takes around 5 minutes.) Oil the bowl, put the dough back into it, turning to coat it in the oil, then stretch a piece of plastic wrap over the top. Let sit until doubled in size: as little as 45 minutes in a warm room; 2 hours or more in a cold place; or overnight in the fridge. Then punch the dough down and let rise again. It will be quicker this time – but if you're not ready to use it, you can punch it down again, and put it into the fridge or freezer to use later.

If you wish to bake the pizza at this point, set the oven to 400°F. Lightly oil two large cookie sheets. Take a quarter of the pizza dough and roll it out into a thin circle about 12 inches across; or take an eighth of the mixture and make an 8-inch circle, or whatever size you prefer. Transfer to an oiled cookie sheet. Add your chosen topping (see suggestions below) and bake for 15-20 minutes, or until the pizza is crisp at the edges, the dough is cooked right through in the center, and the top is lightly browned. It's wonderful straight from the oven, but also good warm or cold.

Pizza Toppings

Giardinara

A favorite with all the children – everyone, really. Spread the rolled-out dough with Tomato Sauce (p. 92). Homemade is best, but a good one from a jar will do, or even just canned tomatoes, drained, seasoned and chopped. Then top with frozen or drained canned corn; thinly sliced onion, green or red bell pepper, and small white mushrooms; and thin stems of asparagus, if liked. Sprinkle grated cheese all over the top or drizzle with olive oil (the cheese is oily enough on its own).

Tomato and Onion

Spread thinly with tomato sauce, as above, then top with thinly sliced mild onion (red onion, which looks pretty; or Spanish, for a sweet, oniony topping). A few black olives are nice on this, too.

Red Bell Pepper and Olive

Brush the top of the pizza with olive oil, or cover with tomato sauce as before, then top with thin slices of red bell pepper – or red and yellow bell pepper, and some black and/or green olives.

GARLIC

Brush with olive oil, then top with 2-3 finely chopped or thinly sliced garlic cloves. Make 3-4 cuts in the top of the pizza. This one is good served as an accompaniment to a thick soup, casserole, or salad.

PASTA

I usually allow about 1 cup (4 ounces) of dried pasta per person and 4 cups of water per portion of pasta. Cook the pasta in boiling water for about 10 minutes, or until it is tender but still has some bite to it.

Although pasta can always be served simply (with olive oil and garlic, and maybe some slivers of Parmesan; or with a good bought pesto; or just with skinned tomatoes, olive oil, and slivered garlic) one or two good sauces in the freezer never go amiss. Basic Tomato (p. 92), of course, is always useful and can be jazzed up with sliced mushrooms or fresh basil; the Broccoli and Corn Pie Filling (p. 130) also makes a good pasta sauce, as does the Mushroom Pie Filling (p. 131). Here are two more for the freezer, plus a quick zucchini one.

BROCCOLI CREAM SAUCE*

This is delicious made with broccoli but you could use other vegetables instead – just cut them into reasonably sized pieces, cook them lightly, and add to the cream sauce. Asparagus is especially good in the summer.

SERVES 4 ADULTS

2 tablespoons butter or pure vegetable margarine
1 onion, peeled and finely chopped
1 garlic clove, peeled and minced
1 $1/4$ cups light cream or soy cream
12 ounces broccoli, washed and cut into fairly small pieces

1 teaspoon cornstarch
salt and freshly ground black pepper
grated nutmeg

Melt the butter or margarine in a small saucepan and add the onion and garlic; cover and cook gently until the onion is tender but not brown – 5-10 minutes. Then pour in most of the cream, keeping enough back to make a paste with the cornstarch. Let simmer gently for about 5 minutes, until the cream has thickened a bit. To stabilize it, blend the cornstarch with the remaining cream and add. Stir until the sauce has thickened even more, let cook for 1 minute, then remove from the heat.

Meanwhile cook the broccoli in a little boiling water until just tender – check after 3-4 minutes. Drain and add to the sauce, with salt, pepper, and nutmeg to taste. Use right away on freshly cooked pasta; or cool, put into suitable covered containers, and freeze until required. To use, thaw, then reheat gently.

MEDITERRANEAN SAUCE*

This goes well with a chunky pasta such as penne rigate.

SERVES 4 ADULTS

2 tablespoons olive oil
1 onion, peeled and chopped
1 garlic clove, peeled and minced
1 red bell pepper, seeded and chopped
1 eggplant, cut into $^1/_4$-inch dice
14-ounce can tomatoes
salt and freshly ground black pepper

Heat the oil in a fairly large saucepan, and put in the onion, garlic, red bell pepper, and eggplant. Stir, cover, and let cook gently for 10 minutes.

Then add the tomatoes, breaking them up with a wooden spoon. Bring to a boil, and let simmer gently, uncovered, until all the liquid has disappeared: 15-20 minutes. Season with salt and pepper.

Use right away on freshly cooked pasta, or cool, put into suitable covered containers, and freeze until required. To use, thaw, then reheat gently.

ZUCCHINI, PARSLEY, AND LEMON SAUCE

This sauce goes particularly well with fusilli. Although it cannot be frozen, it's very quick and easy to make, and best eaten straight away.

SERVES 2-4 ADULTS

**2 tablespoons olive oil
12 ounces zucchini, thinly sliced
rind of 1 lemon, pared with a zester or grated
juice of $^1/_2$ lemon
2 tablespoons chopped fresh parsley
salt and freshly ground black pepper**

While the pasta is cooking, heat the oil in a large saucepan, then put in the zucchini, stir, cover, and let cook gently until just tender. Look at the zucchini after 5 minutes – they may need a bit longer. Remove from the heat and add the lemon rind and juice, the parsley, and salt and pepper to taste. Drain the pasta and return it to the still-warm saucepan. Add the zucchini and lemon mixture to the pasta, along with the chopped parsley, and mix. Check the seasoning, and serve.

BREAD, CAKES, & SWEET SNACKS

MOLASSES OAT BARS*

These healthy oat bars, sometimes called blackjacks, are made with molasses or black treacle for extra iron, calcium, and B vitamins. Use ordinary rolled oats, not the 'jumbo' type from health food stores as they are too chewy for this recipe which is quite chewy enough as it is.

MAKES 16 FLAPJACKS

$1/4$ **cup molasses or black treacle**
$1/4$ **cup brown sugar**
8 tablespoons peanut or soybean oil
3 cups rolled oats
$1/2$ **cup sunflower seeds**

Set the oven to 350°F. Put the molasses or treacle, the sugar, and oil into a medium saucepan and heat gently. When the sugar has dissolved, remove from the heat and stir in the oats and sunflower seeds. Put the mixture into a greased shallow cake pan, 7 x 11 inches, press down, and bake towards the top of the oven for 20-25 minutes, or until set, crisp round the edges, and the visible oats are golden brown. Cool slightly, then mark into sections with a knife and leave in the cake pan to cool completely.

Easy Molasses Bread*

This bread is made by the quick one-rise method, which does not require any kneading. I like to add blackstrap molasses, which gives it a slight sweetness and also makes it more nutritious.

MAKES 3 LARGE (2-POUND) LOAVES

butter or pure vegetable margarine
13 cups whole wheat flour
1 slightly heaping tablespoon salt
2 packets instant yeast
1 slightly heaping tablespoon molasses

Grease three large bread pans– or the equivalent, including cake pans, if you wish – generously with butter or margarine. Tip the flour and salt into a large bowl and add the yeast. Mix gently. Dissolve the molasses in a little tepid water taken from $6^1/4$ cups. Add this to the flour, then mix in the rest of the water, going carefully at the end in case you don't need quite all of it. The finished mixture needs to be too wet to leave the sides of the bowl clean; it should feel 'slippery' but not completely sloppy. Half-fill the pans with the mixture, cover them with plastic wrap or a damp dish towel, and leave to rise.

Meanwhile set the oven to 400°F. When the loaves have risen to within $1/2$ inch of the tops of the pans, put them in the oven. Bake large loaves for 45 minutes, and small ones for about 35 minutes, or until they are brown and firm to the touch, and sound hollow when you slip them out of the pans and tap them on the base with your knuckles. If you wish, you can crisp the base and sides a bit more by putting the loaves back into the oven for a few minutes after you've taken them out of the pans. Cool the bread on a wire rack.

FRUIT CAKE

3 cups whole wheat flour
1 teaspoon ground mixed spices (cloves, nutmeg, cinnamon)
^{2}/$_3$ cup peanut oil
^{3}/$_4$ cup dark brown (molasses) sugar
1^1/$_3$ cups currants, raisins, and/or other dried fruit
^{2}/$_3$ cup candied cherries, rinsed and halved
grated rind of 1 well-scrubbed orange
^{1}/$_4$ cup ground almonds
^{1}/$_2$ cup milk or soy milk
2 tablespoons vinegar
^{3}/$_4$ teaspoon baking soda

Set the oven to 300°F. Grease an 8-inch cake pan and line with a double layer of wax paper. Sift the flour and spices into a bowl, adding the bran from the sifter, too. Stir in the peanut oil, brown sugar, dried fruit, candied cherries, orange rind, and ground almonds and mix until combined. Warm half the milk in a small saucepan and add the vinegar. Dissolve the baking soda in the rest of the milk, then add to the milk and vinegar mixture and pour into the flour and fruit, blending well. Spoon into the prepared cake pan. Bake for 2-2^1/$_2$ hours, until a cake tester inserted into the center of the cake comes out clean. Leave to cool in the pan, then strip off the wax paper.

NUTTY CAROB BANANAS*

These are rather like healthy ice creams. If you are giving them to young children, either use very finely chopped nuts or leave the nuts out.

liquid honey
carob powder
finely chopped mixed nuts
1 banana per person, peeled and cut into 3 equal pieces

Put the honey, carob powder, and chopped nuts on three saucers. Dip each piece of banana first into the honey, then into the carob powder, and finally into the nuts, so that it is well coated. Put the banana pieces onto a flat plate or cookie sheet and freeze until solid – this will take about 2 hours or more. Eat straight from the freezer. You can insert Popsicle sticks into the pieces of banana before freezing, if you like.

FRUIT AND NUT BARS*

These healthy bars are especially rich in calcium, iron, and B vitamins. They make an ideal snack for toddlers and for pregnant or breastfeeding moms. Once made, the bars can be frozen. Take out individually as required: they can be eaten within a few minutes.

MAKES 16 BARS

$1/2$ cup dried apricots
1 cup dates
1 cup dried figs
2-3 tablespoons orange juice
$3/4$ cup unsweetened shredded coconut
$1/2$ cup ground almonds
grated rind of 1 orange or lemon
extra unsweetened shredded coconut

Wash the apricots thoroughly, then chop all the dried fruit – a food processor is good for this. Then add the orange juice, coconut, almonds, and grated rind. Press the mixture into a lightly greased 8-inch square shallow cake pan, making it about $^1/_2$ inch deep. Sprinkle with more shredded coconut. Chill, then cut into bars.

PARKIN*

Taken from my book *Complete Vegetarian Cuisine*, this has always been a favorite with my children – a sweet treat that is nourishing as well as good to eat. It gets stickier if you keep it for a few days, wrapped in aluminum foil.

MAKES 12-16 PIECES

1 cup whole wheat flour
2 teaspoons baking powder
2 teaspoons ground ginger
1 $^1/_3$ cups rolled oats
$^1/_2$ cup dark brown (molasses) sugar
$^1/_2$ cup black molasses
$^1/_2$ cup honey or corn syrup
$^1/_2$ cup butter or pure vegetable margarine
$^3/_4$ cup milk or soy milk

Set the oven to 350°F. Line an 8-inch square cake pan with wax paper. Sift the whole wheat flour, baking powder, and ground ginger into a bowl, adding the bran left in the sifter, and also the rolled oats. Now put the sugar, molasses, honey or corn syrup, and butter or margarine into a saucepan and heat gently until melted. Let cool until you can comfortably put your hand against the saucepan, then add the milk or soy milk. Add this mixture to the dry ingredients, mixing well, and pour into the prepared cake pan. Bake for 50-60 minutes, until firm to the touch. Lift the parkin out of the cake pan and put on a wire rack to cool, then cut into pieces and remove from the paper.

PUDDINGS, COMPOTES, & DESSERTS

RHUBARB CRUMBLE*

This is so popular with children, as well as being easy to make, that it *had* to be included. It comes from my book *Complete Vegetarian Cuisine*.

SERVES 4 ADULTS OR 6 CHILDREN

2 pounds rhubarb, cut into 1-inch lengths
1 cup sugar
2 cups self-rising brown or whole wheat flour
³/4 cup butter or pure vegetable margarine

Set the oven to 400°F. Put the rhubarb into a lightly greased large shallow ovenproof dish. Mix in ¹/3 cup of the sugar; make sure that the fruit is in an even layer. Put the flour into a bowl and rub in the butter with your fingertips until the mixture looks like fine bread crumbs and there are no obvious bits of fat showing. Add the remaining sugar and mix gently. Spoon the crumble topping all over the rhubarb in an even layer. Bake for 30-40 minutes, until the crumble is crisp and lightly browned and the fruit feels tender when pierced with the point of a knife. You could add some slivered almonds to the crumble mix for extra nutrients.

VARIATION

Or you could use another crumble, which is based on one of Peter Cox's iron-boosting ideas from *The Encyclopaedia of Vegetarian Living* and is also good as a granola for breakfast, or as an iron-rich nibble during the day. The whole quantity supplies around 25 mg of iron.

$^1/_4$ **cup sunflower seeds**
$^1/_4$ **cup sesame seeds**
$^1/_4$ **cup pumpkin seeds**
$^1/_2$ **cup pistachios or slivered almonds**
$^2/_3$ **cup rolled oats**
1 tablespoon molasses
$^1/_2$ **teaspoon vanilla extract**

Set the oven to 400°F. Mix all the ingredients together in a bowl and then spread out the lumpy mixture on a cookie sheet. Bake for 20-30 minutes, stirring several times so that it cooks evenly. Remove from the oven and let cool and become crisp. I think it's nice with a few raisins tossed in after it's cooled – and these add even more iron.

RICE PUDDING

Nothing would make me eat rice pudding as a child, but now I think it's one of the most comforting puddings. It's good hot or cold and can be made richer by adding cream or soy cream and chopped dried or candied fruits and nuts – pistachios are especially good. My children all loved it.

SERVES 2-3 ADULTS OR 4-5 CHILDREN

2 tablespoons butter or pure vegetable margarine
^{1}/2 cup round-grain 'pudding' rice
4 tablespoons brown sugar
5 cups milk or soy milk
freshly grated nutmeg

Set the oven to 325°F. Use the butter or margarine to grease a shallow ovenproof dish. Rinse the rice thoroughly under cold running water, then put it into the dish with the sugar and milk or soy milk; stir gently. Grate some nutmeg on top, then place in the center of the oven and bake for about 2 hours, or until thick and creamy.

MILLET AND RAISIN CREAM

The old-fashioned milk puddings that our grandmothers used to make were nutritionally excellent, as well as economical. This up-to-date version is based on protein- and iron-rich flaked millet, with raisins for sweetness.

SERVES 3 ADULTS OR 4-5 CHILDREN

^{1}/2 cup flaked millet
2 cups milk or soy milk
^{1}/3 cup raisins
grated lemon rind (optional)
1-2 tablespoons honey (optional)

Put all the ingredients into a saucepan and bring to a boil. Reduce the heat to as low as possible and let simmer very gently for 20-30 minutes, or until it has thickened. The mixture can be served hot or poured into individual serving dishes and let cool. It's good with some light cream or thick plain yogurt on top.

BAKED APPLES WITH RAISINS

Easy, nutritious, and delicious served with some chilled plain yogurt.

SERVES 4 ADULTS OR CHILDREN

4 medium-size cooking apples
$^1/_3$ cup raisins

Set the oven to 400°F. Wash the apples and remove the cores, then score around the center of each with a sharp knife, just piercing the skin to prevent them from bursting as they cook. Place the apples in an ovenproof dish, fill the centers with the raisins, and bake for 45 minutes or until the apples are tender.

BAKED PEACHES

Halve ripe (unpeeled) peaches, one per person, and remove the pits. Put them, cut-side down, in a buttered baking dish and sprinkle with demerara sugar. Bake at 350°F for about 25 minutes, until they can be pierced easily with a knife. Alternatively, put them in the baking dish the other way up and stuff the cavities with a mixture of crushed macaroons and port or marsala, sweetened with a little sugar if you wish. Don't cover them; bake as before.

Once the port or marsala has been cooked, it becomes non-alcoholic. However, if you prefer to avoid alcohol, substitute some orange juice.

BAKED BANANAS

Simply put whole, unpeeled bananas in a baking pan and bake at 350°F until you can pierce them easily with a knife – about 25-30 minutes. Serve immediately. Thick yogurt or vanilla ice cream also goes well with them. For a more luxurious version, remove a section of skin from the top of each banana before baking, make some cuts in the banana, and insert some slim squares of chocolate. Bake as before. Again, excellent with vanilla ice cream – or whipped cream.

APPLES WITH RAISINS*

In this recipe the raisins add extra food value (iron and B vitamins) as well as sweetness, so that little or no extra sweetening is needed. If this is sieved or pureed after cooking, it makes an excellent dessert for babies. To freeze, let cool quickly, spoon into a suitable covered container, and place in the freezer. Before use, let thaw for several hours at room temperature, then either heat gently or serve cold with some light cream.

SERVES 4 ADULTS

2 tablespoons butter or pure vegetable margarine
2 pounds dessert apples, peeled, cored, and sliced
¹/₃ cup raisins
honey (optional)

Melt the butter or margarine in a heavy-bottomed saucepan and add the apples and raisins. Stir, cover, and cook gently for about 10 minutes, or until the apples are soft. Stir from time to time to prevent it burning.

VARIATION
This is equally good made with dates instead of raisins. Use cooking dates (not sugar-rolled) and check that the pits have been removed.

Molasses Compote

This compote is based on an idea in Peter Cox's invaluable *Encyclopaedia of Vegetarian Living*. Eaten 2-3 times a day, it can supply up to 20 mg of iron, so it can be very useful just after the birth. I find this a pleasant way to take iron: it tastes much better than it sounds!

²/₃ cup each of dried figs, apricots, dates, and prunes or dried peaches
1 tablespoon blackstrap molasses
1 tablespoon crushed pistachio nuts

Wash the fruit and put it into a bowl. Dissolve the molasses in some boiling water and pour it over the fruit, adding more water so that the fruit is covered. Leave for at least 12 hours; it will keep for several days, covered, in the fridge. Serve with the pistachios on top.

VARIATIONS

DRIED FRUIT COMPOTE
If intensive iron-boosting isn't your main concern, you could leave out (or reduce) the molasses and add some slivers of lemon rind to the mixture. You could also replace some of the water with fresh fruit juice.

DRIED AND FRESH FRUIT COMPOTE
Make as above, either with or without molasses, and add some fresh fruit before serving: sections of orange, with the pith cut away, are good; so are slices of kiwi fruit, apple, and banana.

FRESH FRUIT IDEAS

LITCHIS AND KIWI FRUIT

Remove the shell-like skin from the litchis (or use canned litchis) and mix with slices of skinned kiwi fruit. Slices of orange or satsuma are good, too.

EXOTIC FRUIT

Mix together two or more types, depending on what you like, what is available, and what is really ripe: juicy mango, papaya, and persimmon are all good. I prefer canned guavas to fresh – these could be added, too, and some pretty cape gooseberries, with the dried sepals pulled back like petals.

BIG C FRUIT SALAD

This refreshing fruit salad or starter can give you a vitamin C boost of about 300 mg. You could increase the vitamin C further by adding sliced red bell pepper (just 4 ounces will give you around another 200 mg of vitamin C) and/or Belgian endive, which is also an excellent source of this vitamin.

SERVES 1

1 orange
1 grapefruit
1 kiwi fruit

Cut the peel from the orange and grapefruit and remove the flesh from the sections, holding the fruit over a bowl to catch all the juice. Thinly peel the kiwi fruit, then slice that into the bowl too. Mix and serve.

FIGS WITH YOGURT AND SESAME SEEDS

This useful dessert or breakfast dish supplies over half the recommended daily calcium allowance during pregnancy. Simply mix
$^2/_3$ cup of chopped dried figs with $^2/_3$ cup of plain dairy or vitamin-enriched soy yogurt, and then sprinkle over 1 heaping tablespoon sesame seeds.

SLICED PEACHES IN WINE

Cover ripe peaches with boiling water for 1 minute, or until the skin loosens, then slip the skin off, halve, pit, and thinly slice the peaches. Put them into a bowl, sprinkle with white wine and a little sugar, and let sit for a few hours before serving. Nectarines are good prepared like this, too. If you wish to avoid wine, you can use orange juice instead, and omit the sugar.

APRICOT FOOL

This is easy to make and rich in both iron and calcium – an excellent pudding for babies if you omit the almonds.

SERVES 3 ADULTS OR CHILDREN

1 $1/3$ cups dried apricots
1 cup thick creamy yogurt or soy yogurt
liquid honey or demerara sugar
slivered almonds (optional)

Cover the apricots with boiling water and let soak overnight. The next day, simmer for 20-30 minutes, or until tender. Cool, then puree in a food processor. Fold the yogurt or soy yogurt into the apricot puree and sweeten with honey or sugar to taste. Serve in small bowls with some slivered almonds on top. If you wish, you can make this creamier by replacing some of the yogurt with whipped cream.

VARIATIONS

For Mango Fool, use a very ripe mango. Remove the pit, peel, and puree the flesh. Mix with yogurt, soy yogurt, or yogurt and cream as above. Alternatively, to make Blackberry Fool, just mash very ripe blackberries and fold into yogurt, or yogurt and cream, as above.

FRESH FRUIT WITH APRICOT SAUCE

This sauce is delicious with slices of fresh fruit – apples, pears, oranges, bananas – and provides useful iron, vitamin A, and calcium. Soak and cook dried apricots as for Apricot Fool (p. 149). Then puree them, adding enough of their liquid to get a pouring consistency.

BANANAS WITH GINGER

Peel and slice fresh bananas; top with a little chopped candied ginger, a spoonful of the ginger syrup, and perhaps a few crushed nuts.

HEALTHY ICE CREAM[★]

All children love this. It freezes very hard so it needs to be left at room temperature for 45-60 minutes.

SERVES 8 CHILDREN

$2^3/4$ cups milk or soy milk
4 squares of bittersweet chocolate, broken into pieces
2 slightly heaping tablespoons sugar
1 tablespoon cornstarch
14-ounce can evaporated milk or soy cream

Put all but 4 tablespoons of the milk into a large saucepan with the chocolate and sugar and bring slowly to a boil. In a bowl, mix the cornflour to a paste with the remaining milk. Add a little of the boiling milk to the cornstarch mixture, stir, then pour the mixture into the hot milk. Stir over the heat for 2-3 minutes, until it has thickened a little, then remove from the heat. Add the evaporated milk or soy cream and blend until smooth. Pour into a plastic container, cool completely, and freeze until half set. Beat well, and freeze until firm.

Useful Addresses

American College of Nurse-Midwives (ACNM)
818 Connecticut Avenue, NW, Suite 900,
Washington, DC 20006
Tel: (202) 728-9860
Provides brochures and referrals for accredited nurse-midwives.

American Dietetic Association
216 West Jackson Boulevard, Chicago, IL 60606
Tel: 1-800-366-1655
Provides information on registered dietitians, including those with specialties in vegetarianism and maternal care. Also a source of brochures and nutritional factsheets on the different types of vegetarian diets.

American Vegan Society
56 Dinshaw Lane, PO Box H, Milaga, NJ 08328-0908
Tel: (609) 694-2887
Cookbooks, videos, and nutritional information related to the vegan diet. They also publish *Ahimsa*, a quarterly magazine.

Depression After Delivery (DAD)
PO Box 1282, Morrisville, PA 19067
Tel: (215) 295-3994
Support, information, and referral to women and families suffering from post-partum depression.

Healthy Mothers, Healthy Babies Coalition
409 12th Street, SW Washington, DC 20004-2188
Tel: (202) 638-5577
Affiliated with the American College of Obstetricians and Gynecologists (ACOG), this organization refers pregnant women and new mothers to the local group that best serves their individual needs.

International Childbirth Education Association
PO Box 20048, Minneapolis, MN 55420-0048
Tel: (612) 854-8660; (800) 624-4934 to order books
Provides literature on pregnancy and childbirth.

La Leche League International
1400 North Meacham Road, PO Box 4079,
Schaumburg, IL 60168-4079

Tel: (847) 519-7730 for catalogue and new mother packet; (800) LA-LECHE for specific questions and referral to local leaders
Information and support for nursing mothers and referral to local La Leche leaders.

National Maternal and Child Health Clearinghouse
2070 Chain Bridge Road, Suite 450, Vienna,
VA 22182
Tel: (703) 821-7098
A source of booklets and products for new and expecting mothers.

National Women's Health Network
514 10th Street, NW, Suite 400, Washington, DC 20004
Tel: (202) 628-7814
Clearinghouse agency which publishes 75 low-cost information packets on women's health issues, including pregnancy and childbirth, and also gives information on local clinics and resource centers.

North American Vegetarian Society
PO Box 72, Dolgeville, NY 13329
Tel: (518) 568-7970
Booklets, outreach efforts, support services for vegetarians. They also publish a quarterly news magazine, *Vegetarian Voice*.

Sudden Infant Death Syndrome Alliance
1314 Bedford Avenue, Suite 210, Baltimore,
MD 21208
Tel: (800) 638-SIDS
Pamphlets on preventive care for new and expectant families as well as a counseling service for bereaved families.

Vegetarian Awareness Network (VEGANET)
Box 321, Knoxville, TN 37901
Tel: (800) 872-8343
Free recipes and referrals to local groups as well as environmental and nutritional information.

Vegetarian Resource Group
PO Box 1463, Baltimore, MD 21203
Tel: (410) 366-8343
Vegetarian recipes and literature, including a booklet on "The Vegan Diet During Pregnancy, Lactation, and Childbirth" and a magazine, *Vegetarian Journal*.

Further Reading

Birth Over Thirty by Sheila Kitzinger (New York: Penguin, 1985)

Breastfeeding Your Baby by Sheila Kitzinger (New York: Knopf, 1989)

Breastfeeding: Getting Breastfeeding Right For You by Mary Renfrew, Chloe Fisher, and Suzanne Arms (Berkeley: Celestial Arts, 1990)

The Complete Book of Pregnancy and Childbirth by Sheila Kitzinger (New York: Knopf, 1996)

The Experience of Breastfeeding by Sheila Kitzinger (New York: Penguin, 1987)

Good Food Today, Great Kids Tomorrow by Jay Gordon and Antonia B. Boyle (Studio City: Wiese, 1994)

Pregnancy, Children, and the Vegan Diet by Michael Klaper, MD (Felton, CA: Gentle World, 1988)

Raising Your Family Naturally by Joy Gross (New York: Carol, 1988)

Vegetarian Baby: A Sensible Guide for Parents by Sharon Yntema (Ithaca: McBooks, 1980)

Vegetarian Child by Joy Gross and Karen Freifeld (New York: Carol, 1983)

Vegetarian Children: A Supportive Guide for Parents by Sharon Yntema (Ithaca: McBooks, 1995)

Vegetarian Pregnancy: The Definitive Nutritional Guide to Having a Healthy Baby (Ithaca: McBooks, 1994)

Your Baby and Child by Penelope Leach (New York: Knopf, 1989)

For more quick, nutritious vegetarian recipes which are enjoyed by children as well as adults, see these other Rose Elliot books: *The Classic Vegetarian Cookbook* (Dorling Kindersley, 1994), *The Complete Vegetarian Cuisine* Pantheon, 1997), *Rose Elliot's Vegetarian Christmas* (HarperCollins San Francisco, 1993), *Vegetarian Dishes from Around the World* (Pantheon, 1982), *Vegetarian Fast Food* (Random House 1995), *Vegetarian Four Seasons* (Random House, 1994)

General Index

Recipe Index